NYC For Free

First Edition

Tatra Press

New York

Library of Congress Catalog Card Number: 98-90099

ISBN: 09661847-0-X

Writer: Christopher C. Sulavik
Editors: Stephen B. Sulavik, Emily R. Church
Designer: Nancy Gonzalez
Publisher: Tatra Press, 111 Congress St., Brooklyn, NY 11201

Printed in the United States of America

Table of Contents

Foreword 5
Alternative Spaces 6
Auction Houses 9
Beaches 11
Cemeteries 13
Classical Music 15
Comedy 20
Cultural Centers 21
Cultural Information 24
Dance Clubs and Lounges (No Cover DJ) 26
Dance Performances 28
Film 30
Galleries 32
Gardens 47
Gay/Lesbian 50
Happy Hours (with free appetizers) 52
Health Services 55
Jazz, Rock & Folk Music 60
Lectures 67
Libraries 71
Literary Events 74
Meditation 79
Museums 81
NYC Web Sites 92
Outdoor Performances 94
Parks 99
Pets 101
Piano Bars 102
Places for Children 107
Publications 111
Religious Buildings 113

Resources for the Disabled 115
Restful Places 117
Societies & Institutes 120
Theater 127
Tours 130
TV Shows 134
Victims' Services 137
Wildlife 139
Women's Groups 141
Zoos 143
Miscellaneous 144
Festivals, Fairs & Parades Calendar 146

Foreword

It takes effort to avoid financial leakage in this City, and obsessing on bargains can often ruin what should be a nice time out. This book is meant to ease that burden by pointing you to some of the City's most impressive free events and services.

When making our selections, we had many people in mind: weekend visitors cash-strapped hours after arriving; tourists on cold, rainy days ducking into diners for a warm place to regroup; dissatisfied theater goers at intermission wondering if their $60 ticket should have been worth less. We see this book as a list of things we would jot down if tipped, or tear out of the paper.

Included are well over 600 items in 41 categories, concentrated on entertainment and the arts. We have also attempted to cast light on other more serious services like H.I.V. screenings, outreach hotlines and research libraries. The breadth of listings should, therefore, be useful to both residents and visitors.

Mostly, we've avoided being too enthusiastic or dour in our comments. We urge readers of this book to use the phone numbers provided throughout. Information becomes obsolete very quickly in this City and, by calling first, you can also get a feeling whether the place or event will suit you.

We must note that while every effort was made to ensure the accuracy of each listing, there may, however, be inaccuracies, both typographical and in content. Therefore, please use this book as a general guide, rather than an ultimate source for information.

Alternative Spaces

New York has seen a flourishing of alternative spaces over the last two decades, especially Downtown. Alternative spaces can mean many things. Some offer performances, video presentations, installations, gallery spaces, or a combination of all of these. Those selected here (to varying degrees) hold exhibitions and performances open free to the public. However, the term alternative space is slowly becoming a bit of a misnomer. White Columns, Exit Art and Thread Waxing Space, for example, have grown from obscure to nationally-recognized institutions, becoming not merely alternative, but musts for art lovers. More are cropping up, all striving to nurture new art media and fresh talent.

Call or stop by to get a feel for the nature and attitude of the different spaces, because there's an extraordinary range.

Art in General

Address: 79 Walker Street (between Broadway and Lafayette)
Open: Tuesday through Saturday, Noon to 6:00 pm
Phone: (212) 219-0473
Comments: This non-profit organization, housed in the General Tools warehouse building in TriBeCa, has given many emerging, lesser-known artists their first exhibition. It specializes in mixed media, video and installations showcased in its two galleries on the fourth and sixth floors. Even the elevator is filled with young artists' "audio projects."

Artists Space

Address: 38 Greene Street
Open: Tuesday through Sunday, 10:00 am to 6:00 pm
Phone: (212) 226-3970
Comments: Founded in 1973, this space shows video and performance art, architecture and design. Widely used by alternative artists, the space presents film, mixed media and lectures. Hosts regular "video calls," a compilation of videos submitted by local artists. The space also houses a library of slides on art works by about 3,500 artists in New York State for viewing.

DIA Center for the Arts

Address: 548 West 22nd Street (between Tenth and Eleventh Avenues)
Open: Thursday through Sunday, Noon to 6:00 pm
Phone: (212) 989-5912
Comments: A large, major contemporary art museum, the Center presents changing exhibitions on many established artists, and showings have included works by Andy Warhol and Walter de Maria. Exhibits are usually shown for up to a year and are often quite large installations. Also sponsors "Readings in Contemporary Poetry" series with acclaimed poets and dance performances, some free. Call for details. (The Center plans to open another space to house its permanent collection at 535 West 22nd Street in 1998).

Exit Art

Address: 548 Broadway (between Prince and Spring Streets)
Open: Tuesday through Thursday, 10:00 am to 6:00 pm; Friday, 10:00 am to 8:00 pm; Saturday and Sunday, Noon to 6:00 pm
Phone: (212) 966-7745
Comments: With 17,000 square feet, Exit Art serves as a gallery and place for artists to work. Shows embrace a wide range including mixed media, sculpture, video, performance art and theater. A recent show, entitled "La Traditione," displayed works progressing to completion day by day.

P.S. 1 Museum

Address: 22-25 Jackson Avenue, Long Island City, Queens
Open: Wednesday through Sunday, Noon to 6:00 pm
Phone: (718) 784-2084
Comments: Billed as one of New York's oldest alternative spaces, and unquestionably the largest — at 125,000 feet — P.S. 1 hosts lectures, changing exhibitions, opening celebrations and programs for artists. Home to cutting- edge visual and performing art for over 30 years, this space has become a vibrant laboratory for innovative art, and is a must stop when in Queens. It is mostly known for large-scale installations.

Storefront for Art and Architecture

Address: 97 Kenmare (between Cleveland and Mulberry Streets)
Open: Tuesday through Saturday, 11:00 am to 6:00 pm
Phone: (212) 431-5795
Comments: Housed in a building of architectural curiosity itself, the space is dedicated to art on architecture including drawings, paintings and other art forms. The non-profit gallery also hosts lectures and sym-

posia as well as an occasional design competition. Exhibits "alternative and cutting edge" architectural design.

Thread Waxing Space

Address: 476 Broadway, 2nd floor
Phone: (212) 966-9520
Comments: This non-profit, free-of-charge art gallery opened in 1991 on lower Broadway. A multitude of art forms thrive in this loft space, including film, video, musical performances, installations and performance art. Call for special events free of charge, and times.

White Columns

Address: 154 Christopher Street, 2nd floor
Open: Wednesday through Sunday, Noon to 6:00 pm
Phone: (212) 924-4212
Comments: Founded in 1969, and one of New York's oldest alternative spaces. A haven for new artists, White Columns is a not-for-profit gallery which hosts changing exhibitions of various art forms. Its mission is to encourage young artists, and a criterion to exhibit here is that the artist cannot be represented by a commercial gallery. Shows the work of some 200 visual artists each year to about 1,200 visitors monthly.

Auction Houses

The auction houses selected here welcome visitors to visit previews of sales — as well as to attend the auction — free of charge. While you may intend to bid, there is no pressure to do so. Attending previews is a little like going to a spectacular garage sale, and can approach the satisfaction of visiting some of the City's best museums. The auctions themselves are dramatic events and a bit voyeuristic, if you are not intending to bid. Call or write for upcoming auctions — you are bound to find some niche of interest — whether it be fine art or fossils.

This short list includes the "A" list — Christie's and Sotheby's — and the "B" list, the smaller, lesser known auction houses which are known for holding quality estate sales and special collections with less pomp and formality and lower starting prices in general.

Christie's

Address: 502 Park Avenue (at 59th Street)

219 East 67th Street (Christie's East)

Open: Auction viewings: Monday through Friday, 10:00 am to 5:00 pm; Saturday, 1:00 pm to 5:00 pm; Sunday, 1:00 pm to 5:00 pm

Phone: (212) 546-1000 (Park Avenue); (212) 606-0400 (Christie's East)

Comments: Established in 1776, Christie's holds regular auctions free and open to the public. Located on Park Avenue and the Upper East Side, also known as Christie's East. Call for details on running auctions and viewings.

Doyle William Galleries

Address: 175 East 87th Street (between Lexington and Third)

Phone: (212) 427-2730

Comments: This well-established and respected Upper East Side auction house welcomes the public to its free periodic auctions. Specializes in fine and decorative arts, paintings and books. Exhibition and previewing hours are normally held Saturday through Tuesday for auctions held on Wednesdays and Thursdays. Call for current auction dates and times.

Sotheby's
Address: 1334 York Avenue
Open: Viewings Monday through Saturday, 10:00 am to 5:00 pm; Sunday 1:00 pm to 5:00 pm
Phone: (212) 606-7000
Comments: One of the world's oldest and most important auction houses, Sotheby's auctions are free and open to the public. Known throughout the world for auctioning some of the most precious art collections, it also recently sold a T-Rex. Call for current and upcoming auctions and viewings.

Swann Galleries
Address: 104 East 25th Street
Open: Auctions held on Thursdays, 10:30 am to 5:00 pm
Phone: (212) 254-4710
Comments: One of New York's preeminent auctioneers, Swann deals in rare books, prints, drawings, photographs, rare documents, Hebraica, Judaica and autographs.

Tepper Galleries
Address: 110 East 25th Street
Phone: (212) 677-5300
Comments: At the top of the city's "B List" of auction houses, 60-year-old Tepper specializes in French, English and American antiques as well as paintings, rugs and other items. Estates could include "everything from A to Z." Auctions are usually held two days each week. Call for details.

Beaches

While New York City doesn't exactly conjures up images of relaxing on a seashore, there are a number of fine beaches within striking distance either by car, train, or even subway. Some are more crowded, yet most are worth the trip for people watching, swimming or even surfing. Keep in mind that most have very restricted swimming areas, which is annoying to those used to freer rein and fewer swimmers to contend with. Also, most beaches charge for parking.

Brighton Beach

Address: Off of Ocean Parkway, Brighton Beach, Brooklyn
Open: 10:00 am to 6:00 pm
Phone: (718) 946-1350
Comments: Made famous by playwright Neil Simon, Brighton Beach is now home to a dense Russian immigrant neighborhood. It lends itself to a rich ethnic brew, and its crowds are thick, due to its proximity to Coney Island Beach. Offers free parking, but the lots and sidestreets fill up quickly in the morning.

Coney Island Beach

Address: Between West 37th Street and Ocean Parkway, Brooklyn
Phone: (718) 946-1350
Comments: A Brooklyn treasure, Coney Island is home to Astro Land and perhaps the world's most famous amusement park and hot dogs. The beach, including Brighton Beach, measures some three miles, much of which is hugged by a boardwalk. Popular for July 4th fireworks display. Free parking, but you'll get best spots early in the morning.

Great Kills Park Beach

Address: Gateway National Recreational Area, Staten Island
Phone: (718) 351-6970
Comments: Situated in Staten Island's Great Kills Park, which offers nature trails and athletic fields, this beach tends to be a bit less crowded than other area beaches.

Jones Beach State Park

Address: Wantagh, Long Island
Phone: (516) 785-1600
Comments: Though not in New York City proper, Long Island's Jones Beach State Park is a major draw for city dwellers, and roughly 40 minutes from Manhattan by car (though traffic could easily extend this). Also accessible by train. Its some six miles of beach are clean, as is the water. Also has ball fields, concessions, a restaurant and sufficient lifeguard patrol.

Manhattan Beach

Address: Oriental Blvd. and Irwin Street, Queens
Phone: (718) 946-1373
Comments: Popular spot for picnickers, with calm waters and modest boardwalk.

Orchard Beach

Address: Pelham Bay Park, The Bronx
Phone: (718) 885-2275
Comments: Drawing over 70,000 people on weekends, Orchard Beach is wildly popular among Bronx residents as well as outsiders. The beach spreads just over one mile with relatively calm waters.

Rockaway Beach

Address: Extends from 1st Street to 149th Street, Queens
Phone: (718) 327-7700
Comments: With over six miles of shore and a generous stretch of promenades, this beach is clearly one of the busiest in the City. With concessions, and sometimes turbulent waters.

Cemeteries

New York has a long tradition of spacious and beautifully maintained cemeteries. In the 19th century, Sundays were commonly spent strolling graveyard grounds, and picnics were not unusual. Even today, the older cemeteries and churchyards are used to relax and enjoy the outdoors, especially in a city that offers so little green space. The four selected here are especially beautiful and noteworthy.

Green Wood Cemetery

Address: Described by Fifth Street and McDonald Avenue and 20th to 37th Streets. Main Gate is located at Fifth and 25th Streets, Brooklyn
Open: Open every day from 8:00 am to 4:00 pm
Phone: (718) 768-7300
Comments: Green Wood, which opened its gates in 1840, has long drawn visitors to its beautiful hills and 20 miles of footpaths. It possesses the highest point of elevation in Brooklyn (217 feet), and has a rich, Victorian architectural feel. Some 500,000 people are buried in its 500 acres. Also of special interest are its unique gravesites, reflecting the lives of the dead through creative sculptures and reliefs. Offers complimentary booklet on the cemetery and its trails.

St. Paul's Churchyard

Address: Broadway between Fulton and Vesey Streets
Phone: (212) 602-0874
Comments: A sister church of Trinity Church, St. Paul's also has a placid graveyard amidst the frenetic Wall Street area. Buried here are revolutionary war hero General Richard Montgomery and renown early 19th century actor George Frederick Cooke.

Trinity Church

Address: Corner of Wall Street and Broadway
Open: Church is open from Monday to Friday, 7:00 am to 6:00 pm; Sunday, 12:30 pm to 4:00 pm
Phone: (212) 602-0700
Comments: A needed respite for weary Wall Streeters, and popular stop for tourists, Trinity is one of the City's oldest and historic churches.

The graveyard behind the church is often one of the quietest places in the Wall Street area, and is also of historical interest, with some of New York's and the country's important figures laid to rest here.

Woodlawn

Address: Described by Jerome Avenue, East 233rd Street, Webster Avenue, Bainbridge Avenue and East 211th Street, Bronx

Open: Open daily, 9:00 am to 4:30 pm

Comments: GreenWood's sister cemetery in the Bronx, Woodlawn opened in 1865, and has about 250,000 burial sites amid its tumbling hills and exquisite landscaping. Laid to rest here include: F.W. Woolworth, Joseph Pulitzer and Duke Ellington.

Classical Music

There are many forums offering free classical music in New York. This chapter lists some of the most outstanding examples of concert halls, other venues and music groups which offer free concerts. Juilliard, for example, provides hundreds of free events throughout the year. Churches, too, provide regular programs of free performances. Many of these concerts might include emerging performers, while others will feature established artists. Also, many of these concerts take place in intimate recital halls with serious listeners.

Bronx Symphony Orchestra

Address: Lehman College: Bedford Park Boulevard, West Bronx
Phone: (718) 960-8232
Comments: An extensive menu of classical symphonic performances, some free of charge.

Brooklyn Conservatory of Music

Address: 58 Seventh Avenue, Brooklyn
Open: Monday through Friday, 9:00 am to 9:00 pm; Saturday, 9:00 am to 4:00 pm
Phone: (718) 622-3300
Comments: Occasionally holds free concerts by students and faculty, usually two to three a semester, including chamber music, jazz, and classical. Call or drop by for details.

Cathedral Church of St. John the Divine

Address: Amsterdam Avenue and 112th Street
Open: Daily, 7:00 am to 6:00 pm
Phone: (212) 316-7540
Comments: With construction begun in 1892, and still only about two-thirds complete, this Gothic cathedral is already the world's largest. Stonecutters are still at work, and their stone yard is open to visitors. The famous rose window, at 40 feet in diameter, is made with some 10,000 pieces of glass. Inside, visitors are welcome to enjoy free organ recitals, choral vespers and choral Eucharists.

Church of St. Lukes in the Fields

Address: 487 Hudson Street
Open: Daily, 9:00 am to 5:00 pm
Phone: (212) 924-0562
Comments: Hosts West Village Choral Summer Sing in the summer months, featuring a wide repertoire of choral works. Throughout the year, concerts include 15th and 16th century choral music, as well as concerts with period instruments. Call for details.

Church of the Transfiguration

Address: 1 East 29th Street (between Fifth and Madison)
Open: Daily, 8:00 am to 6:00 pm
Phone: (212) 684-6770
Comments: This well-known church is host to free recitals and tours. Focuses on organ music, with spring and fall concert series. Look out for Tuesday concerts held at 12:30 pm. Call for details. Noted for one of the best organs in the city, a C.B. Fisk.

Columbia University, Miller Theater

Address: 200 Dodge Hall, Broadway and 116th Street
Phone: (212) 854-7799
Comments: Frequent classical music concerts, mostly performed by students, and many free of charge.

Continental Center

Address: 180 Maiden Lane
Phone: (212) 769-7406
Comments: In this Wall Street building lobby, Juilliard students give free concerts — both solo and group — at noon on Mondays and at 12:30 on Tuesdays.

Equitable Center

Address: 787 Seventh Avenue (between 51st and 52nd Streets)
Phone: (212) 544-8884
Comments: The huge lobby of this Midtown office building hosts free concerts by the Equitable Chorus and instrumental music at midday, but call to confirm.

Frick Collection

Adress: 1 East 70th Street
Phone: (212) 288-0700
Comments: Free classical music concerts are offered at this venerated stately museum. Tickets are acquired by writing by the third Monday before the concerts, which are held on Sundays, at 5:00 pm. Two tickets are available to each applicant. These concerts are recorded by WNYC-FM and are broadcast locally and across the country, so be prepared to be extra quiet.

Juilliard School

Address: 144 West 66th Street
Open: September through June
Phone: (212) 769-7406
Comments: Some of the nation's most promising musicians perform free recitals at this renowned music school's Pall Hall and Alice Tully Hall located at Lincoln Center. Free concerts throughout the week, but call to confirm, or ask for the extensive season program. Also hosts "Wednesdays at One" series, when free tickets are distributed, beginning at 12:30 pm. Also, free concerts are given by Juilliard students and faculty at the Museum of Modern Art. (See "Museums" chapter)

Library and Museum of the Performing Arts

Address: 111 Amsterdam Avenue (at 65th Street)
Phone: (212) 870-1630
Comments: For an afternoon infusion of solo and ensemble performances, as well as dance, film, lectures and theatric works, this Lincoln Center offering is an exceptional opportunity. Tickets are required, but are obtainable an hour before performances. Call for details or drop by for the latest monthly bulletin. Generally, events take place in the Bruno Walter Auditorium throughout the week, and are clustered between noon and 3:00 pm and early evening. Also sponsors a reading series of new plays and a lecture series on the performing arts.

Manhattan School of Music

Address: 120 Claremont Avenue
Open: During the academic year
Phone: (212) 749-2802
Comments: MSM's two main orchestras, the Manhattan Symphony and the Manhattan Philharmonic, comprised of student musicians, put on free concerts throughout the school year.

Mannes College of Music

Address: 150 West 85th Street
Phone: (212) 580-0210
Comments: With some 200 free concerts a year, Mannes offers the public a dazzling array of classical music — from solo instrumentalists to symphonies and choruses. Call for upcoming events, or request calendar of events.

New York Philharmonic Park Concerts

Address: Various locations around the city
Phone: (212) 875-5709 (hotline); (516) 475-5610; (516) 451-6260
Comments: The New York Philharmonic offers some concerts at parks and spaces around the City, usually held late July and early August.

St. Patrick's Cathedral

Address: Fifth Avenue (at 50th Street)
Phone: (212) 753-2261
Comments: New York's most well known house of worship, St. Patrick's is also one the country's most impressive examples of Gothic architecture. Cathedral choir sings Sundays, 10:15 am, as well as occasional organ recitals and chamber music, usually scheduled for Sunday afternoons. Call for event information.

St. Paul's Chapel

Address: Broadway and Fulton Streets
Phone: (212) 602-0847
Comments: Every noon, Monday and Thursday, this landmark chapel — the city's oldest — welcomes visitors for performances of instrumental and choral music (suggested donation of $2).

Third Street Musical School Settlement

Address: 233 East 11th Street
Phone: (212) 777-3240
Comments: This community music school opens its doors for free concerts on Friday nights at 7:30 and on Saturday, during the academic year.

Trinity Church

Address: 74 Trinity Place near Wall Street
Phone: (212) 602-0700 (Concert hot line: (212) 602-0747)
Comments: This lovely brownstone church, one of New York's most

historical, offers concerts usually around 1:00 pm, attracting the Wall Street crowd and a good number of tourists (suggested donations of $2). Keep in mind that the church's small cemetery is also a nice place for reflection.

World Financial Center Arts & Events Program
Address: On Hudson River at north end of Liberty Street
Open: Call for details
Phone: (212) 945-0505
Comments: Most concerts are performed in the World Financial Center's Winter Garden, a colossal three-story atrium with a new set of towering palm trees lined in colonnades. Since 1988, the program has hosted over 700 performances by individual artists and cultural groups. Concerts and performances usually scheduled for 6:00 pm. When weather permits, concerts and performances are held outside the Winter Garden in surrounding plazas. In addition, exhibitions and installations are shown in the Courtyard Gallery, the North Bridge and the Liberty Street Gallery, all public spaces.

World Trade Center
Address: West Street between Vesey and Liberty Streets
Open: July and August, Noon and 5:30 pm
Phone: (212) 435-4170
Comments: Austin J. Plaza in the world-renown World Trade Center offers a smattering of free events, including CenterStage, in July and August featuring free lunchtime (Noon to 2:00 pm) and evening (5:30 pm to 7:30 pm) performances. In the past: Comedy Tuesdays, Jazz Wednesdays, Modern Thursdays and R&B Fridays as well as the Texaco New York Jazz Festival on weekends in the early afternoon. But one ought to call ahead for details on all performances.

Comedy

Most of the country's important comedians began in New York, and most probably launched their careers in front of audiences which didn't have to pay a cover charge. There are still a few clubs where one can laugh for free, and some are just as much fun as those that charge upwards of $30.

Luna Lounge
Address: 171 Ludlow Street (between Houston and Stanton Streets)
Phone: (212) 260-2323
Comments: Regular no cover stand up comedy at this bustling hub in the Lower East Side, attracts young comics and audience. Known also for regular free bands throughout the week.

New York Comedy Club
Address: 241 East 24th Street (between Second and Third Avenues)
Phone: (212) 696-5233
Comments: Every Monday, Open Night comics perform free of charge.

Solo Arts Club
Address: 36 West 17th Street (between Fifth and Sixth Avenues)
Phone: (212) 463-8732
Comments: Noted for its improvisational performances, Solo Arts Club is a popular Chelsea stage.

Toyota Comedy Festival
Comments: Held in June, this festival draws comics from the four corners of the globe, with performances taking place in numerous venues throughout the city. Look out for listings in newspapers.

Cultural Centers

This chapter includes some of the most important centers of art and culture. Mostly dedicated to one region of the city, cultural sphere or artistic discipline, these centers sponsor events and also act as a sort of clearinghouse for information. Many are focused on research and offer lectures and workshops as well as exhibitions and performances. More important, these centers aim toward building a community around any given mission or pursuit. They are, therefore, well worth visiting or subscribing to their mailing lists for upcoming events, many of which are not widely publicized.

Bronx Council on the Arts

Address: 1738 Hone Avenue, Bronx
Phone: (718) 931-9500
Comments: The officially designated cultural agency of Bronx County, the BCA sponsors a vast number of cultural events, many for free. Included are outdoor family programs at the New York Botanical Garden. Call for upcoming events, or ask to receive season calendars, which include an impressive listing of free events.

Brooklyn Arts Council/BACA Downtown Cultural Center

Address: 195 Cadman Plaza, West Brooklyn
Phone: (718) 625-0080
Comments: This nerve center for Brooklyn's cultural life offers up-to-date listings and information on innumerable performances and events throughout Brooklyn, including many free of charge.

Castillo Cultural Center

Address: 500 Greenwich Street (between Spring and Canal Streets)
Open: Monday through Friday, 10:00 am to 10:00 pm; Saturday and Sunday, 11:00 am to 10:00 pm
Phone: (212) 941-5800
Comments: Dedicated to joining artists and scholars to produce experimental art. Hosts intriguing exhibitions as well as lectures. Also houses a small gallery with historical exhibitions and a theater.

Chinese Information & Cultural Center

Address: 1230 Avenue of the Americas
Open: Monday through Friday, 9:00 am to 6:00 pm
Phone: (212) 373-1800
Comments: This cultural center offers things to do and places to go — much of it free of charge — relating to Chinese culture, art and history. Houses library and periodicals room, an exhibition gallery and a theater.

Franklin H. Williams Caribbean Cultural Center and African Diaspora Institute

Address: 408 West 58th Street (between Ninth and Tenth Avenues)
Phone: (212) 307-7420
Comments: Dedicated to chronicling and encouraging the cultural contributions of those of Caribbean and African descent. Holds regular, changing exhibitions as well as dance, music, gallery talks, films, a research center and workshops, some of which are free and open to the public.

Jamaica Arts Center for the Performing and Visual Arts

Address: 161-04 Jamaica Avenue, Jamaica, Queens
Phone: (718) 658-7400
Comments: The JAC, founded in 1972, is housed in a landmark neo-Renaissance building, and sponsors art exhibitions, performances, workshops, and classes in its dance studios, art galleries and a 75 seat black box theater. The center also supports artists-in-residence programs as well as an artists' co-op. Call for free events and programs.

Korean Cultural Service

Address: 460 Park Avenue (at 57th Street)
Open: Monday through Friday, 9:00 am to 5:00 pm. Gallery open 10:00 am to 4:30 pm
Phone: (212) 759-9550; (212) 593-0742
Comments: Offers changing art shows by Korean as well as non-Korean artists, featuring knot decorative arts, painting and sculpture. Call for information on free performances.

New York Public Library for the Performing Arts

Address: 40 Lincoln Center Plaza (at West 65th Street)
Open: Monday and Thursday, 12:00 pm to 8:00 pm; Tuesday, Wednesday, Friday and Saturday, 12:00 pm to 6:00 pm

Phone: (212) 870-1600

Comments: The NYPL for the Performing Arts is a nerve center for many of the most valuable free events in the city. It serves many purposes, only one being the source of information for the myriad stream of performances, lectures, workshops and exhibitions it sponsors and organizes.

Queens Council on the Arts

Address: 70-01 Park Lane South, Woodhaven, Queens
Open: Monday through Friday, 9:00 am to 5:00 pm
Phone: (718) 647-3377
Comments: Sponsor of a string of free concerts and events in Queens, the Council also has an information hotline with fresh listings of fee-based and free events and tourist services.

Snug Harbor Cultural Harbor

Address: 1000 Richmond Terrace, Staten Island
Open: Grounds open every day, 8:00 am to evening. Most exhibitions, Wednesday to Sunday, Noon to 5:00 pm
Phone: (718) 448-2500
Comments: Now run by the Department of Parks and Recreation, Snug Harbor was once a convalescent home for retired sailors. The grounds are worth a visit alone, with water views and 28 19th century historic Greek Revival, Italinate, Second Empire and Beaux-Arts buildings — including the city's second oldest music hall — on 83 acres. It is now home to several arts groups, which sponsor a long list of cultural events including concerts, art exhibitions, and sculpture shows as well as lectures, tours, workshops and crafts fairs. Many events come with a small suggested fee, but many are also free of charge.

Cultural Information

There are innumerable events which don't receive adequate publicity and are too easily missed, unless you know where to uncover them. This chapter highlights some of the key places to turn to for listings of cultural and artistic events. They're good places to call, or to stop by and get literature on goings-on. Though this seems laborious, the work invested will be well-rewarded — you'll find you will discover events that are rarely advertised through conventional channels.

Bronx Information and Cultural Events

Address: 851 Grand Concourse, Bronx
Phone: (718) 590-3199
Comments: Solid source for latest cultural events and goings-on in The Bronx.

Central Park, The Arsenal

Address: The Arsenal, Central Park
Phone: (212) 360-8111
Comments: A trusty source for events sponsored and organized by the Department of Parks and Recreation, especially those held in Central Park. Knowledgeable, helpful staff and free literature. Information on parks, historic houses, special events and citywide services.

Department of Cultural Affairs

Address: 2 Columbus Circle
Open: Monday through Friday, 9:00 am to 5:00 pm
Phone: (212) 841-4100
Comments: The City's hub for free events. Drop by for listings, or call for particular types of events.

Downtown

Address: Lower Manhattan Cultural Council, 5 World Trade Center, Suite 9235
Phone: (212) 432-0900
Comments: An exhaustive listing of Downtown Manhattan's art and cultural events, Downtown is published October through June and distributed throughout the city and is also available through subscription.

Folk Fone

Phone: (212) 674-2508
Comments: A hotline for the city's listings for folk music and performances, not all of which are free.

League of American Theaters and Producers, Inc.

Address: 226 West 47th Street
Phone: (212) 302-4111
Comments: Dedicated to serving the theater industry, this league also has an information hotline for theater information, as well as a Broadway show ticket-buying service.

Mayor's Office of Film, Theater and Broadcasting

Address: 1697 Broadway, 6th floor (entrance on 53rd Street)
Open: Monday through Friday, 9:00 am to 5:00 pm
Phone: (212) 489-6710
Comments: Provides contacts of studios and filmmakers currently shooting films. While tracking down locations may be nettlesome, it is a calculating way to find when and where Hollywood movie shoots are taking place.

Staten Island Economic Development Corporation

Address: One Edgewater Plaza, Suite 217, Staten Island
Phone: (800) 573-SINY or (718) 442-4356
Comments: A one-stop for a wealth of free events, sites, tours, festivals etc., taking place on Staten Island. Visit the center for brochures, or get on the mailing list. Or call for upcoming events.

Dance Clubs and Lounges (No Cover DJ)

New York offers a dazzling range of clubs and lounges and more are opening as '70s disco nostalgia intensifies. Many DJs are accumulating celebrity status with followings in the same way bands attract groupies. Below lists some of the clubs which offer dancing or lounging to recorded music by established DJs for no cover charge.

Anseo
Address: 126 St. Marks Place (between First Avenue and Avenue A)
Open: 5:00 pm to 4:00 am
Phone: (212) 475-4145
Comments: Small bar with regular free DJ music, featuring techno and drums and base. No dance floor.

Candy Bar & Grill
Address: 131 Eighth Avenue (at 16th Street)
Phone: (212) 229-9702
Comments: A laid-back bar and grill with no cover DJ music.

Den of Thieves
Address: 145 Houston Street (between Eldridge and Forsythe Streets)
Open: Sunday to Thursday, 9:00 pm to 3:00 am; Friday and Saturday, 9:00 pm to 4:00 am
Phone: (212) 477-5005
Comments: Popular for its wide range of music and a menu of DJs for no cover.

E&O
Address: 100 West Houston Street (between Thompson Street and LaGuardia Place)
Phone: (212) 254-7000
Comments: Fashionable dance club featuring noted DJs free of cover with music including funk, house and techno, blues and progressive.

Les Poulets
Address: 16 West 22nd Street (at Fifth Avenue)

Phone: (212) 229-2000
Comments: A multi-floor dance emporium drawing huge crowds, occasionally with cover-free DJ music. Call ahead.

Ludlow Bar

Address: 165 Ludlow Street (between Houston and Stanton Streets)
Open: Monday to Sunday, 6:00 pm to 4:00 am
Phone: (212) 353-0536
Comments: Popular bar featuring no cover DJ music spanning an impressive range. "Officially" no dancing.

NV

Address: 289 Spring Street (at Hudson Street)
Open: Wednesday to Friday, 8:00 pm to 4:30 am; Saturday, 8:00 pm to 4:00 am
Phone: (212) 929-NVNV
Comments: Cover most nights, except Sundays, offers up hip hop, R&B, and techno.

Opium Den

Address: 29 East Third Street (between Bowery and Second Avenue)
Open: 6:00 pm to 4:00 am
Phone: (212) 505-7344
Comments: Popular Lower East Side lounge with no cover DJ music.

The Greatest Bar on Earth

Address: 1 World Trade Center 107th floor, Liberty Street (between West and Church Streets)
Phone: (212) 524-7000
Comments: Located in the World Trade Center, on the 107th floor, this bar offers a broad range of dance music. At the Strato Lounge on Wednesdays, beginning around 9:00 pm.

Void

Address: 16 Mercer Street (at Canal Street)
Open: Wednesday and Thursday, 8:00 pm to 2:00 am; Friday and Saturday, 8:00 pm to 3:00 am
Phone: (212) 941-6492
Comments: A popular Downtown eclectic lounge featuring lots of free DJ music. Features experimental and mostly electronic and techno music.

Dance Performances

Dance groups which perform free to the public are few and far between. Below is a list of some good places to start — with Juilliard and Movement Research being the most generous in their program of free dance performances. The "Outdoor Performances" and "Cultural Centers" chapters also include events and organizations offering free dance performances.

American Museum of Natural History

Address: Central Park West (at 79th Street)
Open: Sunday through Tuesday, Thursday, 10:00 am to 5:45 pm; Wednesday, Friday and Saturday, 10:00 am to 9:00 pm
Phone: (212) 769-5000
Comments: Occasionally opens its doors for free dance performances. Museum is free 5:00 pm to 9:00 pm Fridays and Saturdays.

Danspace

Address: St. Mark's Church, 131 East 10th Street
Phone: (212) 674-8194
Comments: While most dance performances are not free, there is an occasional dance that is. Call for details.

Juilliard School

Address: 144 West 66th Street
Phone: (212) 769-7406
Comments: Drawn from Juilliard's Dance division, some of the nation's most promising dance students present performances mainly at the school's Julliard Theater, located at Lincoln Center. Free performances on occasion. Call for details, or subscribe to the school's mailing list, which includes many dance events as well as music and drama.

Laziza Space

Address: 123 Smith Street, Carroll Gardens, Brooklyn
Phone: (718) 797-3116
Comments: Tucked away in Carroll Gardens, Brooklyn, this unique dance studio offers vibrant contemporary dance, with some performances free of charge. Also invites public to filming sessions of dances.

Has loyal following and attracts visitors from the tri-state region. Call for details on next free event.

Movement Research at Judson Church

Address: 55 Washington Square
Phone: (212) 277-6854
Comments: Every Monday night at 8:00 pm, Movement Research, located on Greenwich Village's Washington Square Park, offers free dance performances. Most dancers are emerging professionals, but there are some students that are selected to take the stage. Depending on who is performing, the house may get packed, so arriving at 7:30 pm is advised. During the winter holidays, there are no concerts.

Washington Square United Methodist Church

Address: 135 West 4th Street
Phone: (212) 777-2528
Comments: This Greenwich Village church has made a name for itself by opening its doors to dance and musical events, some of which are held free of charge.

Young DanceMakers Company

Address: Riverside Park
Phone: (212) 362-4740
Comments: An ensemble of dance students from high schools throughout the City creating and performing new works. Performances are often given to community groups mostly during the summer, and all are free of charge. Also, the group sponsors workshops after performances which include the audience as participants.

Film

Free films are a tough catch. But there are opportunities in this city to see free movies, the most popular being the Bryant Park Summer Film Festival. A few bar/cafés have screenings, as well as the New York Public Library and MOMA (under the pay what you wish policy). Free films are occasionally shown at societies and institutes, too, so it's useful to get calendars of events from those that interest you.

A Different Light

Address: 151 West 19th Street (between Sixth and Seventh Avenues)
Phone: (212) 989-4850
Comments: Shows generally campy films every Sunday night at 7:00 pm on a large television screen in a quiet part of this café/bookstore in Chelsea.

Black Star

Address: 92 Second Avenue (at 5th Street)
Phone: (212) 254-4747
Commnets: An East Village watering hole, Black Star projects free films Sunday nights at 8:30 in its Pseudo Mystical Cinema Series, which includes jazz accompaniment.

Bryant Park Summer Film Festival

Address: 42nd Street between Fifth and Sixth Avenues
Phone: (212) 983-4143
Comments: This recently restored park — now one of Manhattan's most stately spots — is home to free Monday night films — at dusk from June to early September. Features classics like "What Ever Happened to Baby Jane" and "Mr. Smith Goes to Washington," with impressive backdrop of midtown skyscrapers.

Donnell Library Center

Address: 20 West 53rd Street (between Fifth and Sixth Avenues)
Open: Monday, Wednesday, Friday, Noon to 6:00 pm; Tuesday and Thursday, 9:30 am to 8:00 pm; Saturday, 10:00 am to 5:00 pm
Phone: (212) 621-0618

Comments: Part of the New York Public Library, Donnell is one of few places which screen films free of charge on a regular basis. Also holds an annual short film and video competition, as well as readings and concerts.

Internet Cafe
Address: 82 East Third Street
Phone: (212) 614-0747
Comments: Free films screened Sunday evenings at 8:00.

Museum of Modern Art
Address: 11 West 53rd Street
Open: Suggested donation Fridays, 4:30 pm to 8:30 pm only
Phone: (212) 708-9400
Comments: This hub for contemporary art also houses two movie theaters, which show important classic and contemporary films every day. There is no required charge for admission (it is suggested that you pay what you wish) to the museum on Fridays from 5:30 pm to 8:30 pm. Most people respectfully pay something, though it is not absolutely obligatory to do so.

New York Public Library Branches
Phone: (212) 869-8089
Comments: The New York Public Library occasionally shows all types of films free of charge at many of its branches. For example, the 58th Street branch (127 East 58th Street, 212-759-7358) has free movies Friday afternoons at 7:00. Call for details.

Ottendorfer Library
Address: 135 Second Avenue
Phone: (212) 674-0947
Comments: Classic children's films for free on Saturdays at 2:00 pm.

Void
Address: 16 Mercer Street
Phone: (212) 941-6492
Comments: Free films every Wednesday evening at 8:30 pm in this Soho bar's "video lounge," a comfortable screening room with a 14-foot screeen.

Galleries

There are too many galleries in New York and the outer boroughs to offer a complete list in this book. This abbreviated selection, however, attempts to provide a visitor or resident with highlights of popular galleries and is restricted to those in Manhattan. The list has been broken into categories — Uptown, Soho/TriBeCa and Greenwich Village — to help organize a trip to several galleries in one area. For the most part, Uptown galleries are those clustered on the Upper East Side, between Madison Avenue and Central Park. Most are commercial galleries, but some institutes and other non-profit organizations are also represented. This list covers a wide range of art and ways of showing it. Note that most galleries are closed on Mondays.

Greenwich Village Area

National Arts Club

Address: 15 Gramercy Park South (between Park Avenue South and Irving Place)
Phone: (212) 475-3424
Comments: A grand 19th century club (early members including Frederic Remington and J. Pierpont Morgan) the National Arts Club is private, but sponsors regular art exhibitions free and open to the public.

New York University, Tracey/Barry Gallery, Fales Library

Address: 70 Washington Square South at LaGuardia Place
Phone: (212) 998-2596
Comments: This small NYU library has hosted some impressive exhibitions, including "Dangerous Pleasures: Classifications and Desire in 18th Century England," a collection of rare books and prints. Call for changing exhibitions and for an appointment.

The Grey Art Gallery and Study Center, New York University

Address: 100 Washington Square East

Open: September though June, Tuesday and Thursday 10:00 am to 6:30 pm; Wednesday and Friday, 10:00 am to 8:30 pm; Saturday 1:00 pm to 5:00 pm. July and August, Monday through Friday, 10:00 to 6:00 pm

Phone: (212) 998-6780

Comments: An important hub for exhibitions of student and established artists in fine arts and multimedia. Also hosts a wide range of events, including lectures, readings and film, many times in collaboration with other institutions. Not all events are free, so call ahead. Recently sponsored "Nahum B. Zenil: Witness to the Self," an exhibition of the Mexican artist.

Visual Arts Museum

Address: 209 East 23rd Street

Phone: (212) 592-2144

Comments: One of the School of Visual Arts' two galleries, sponsors changing art exhibitions, including its annual "Masters Series," which showcases the work of exceptional artists.

Soho/TriBeca

A.I.R. Gallery

Address: 40 Wooster Street, 2nd floor

Open: Tuesday through Saturday, 11:00 am to 6:00 pm

Phone: (212) 966-0799

Comments: Billed as the country's first women artists cooperative, A.I.R is directed and maintained by artists. Its galleries and working spaces provide visitors a glimpse of rising and established women artists.

Ace Gallery New York

Address: 275 Hudson Street
Open: Tuesday through Saturday, 10:00 am to 6:00 pm
Phone: (212) 255-5599
Comments: Focuses on emerging and under-exhibited artists as well as established artists in the following areas: abstract expressive, arte povera, minimal and pop. Most of the work represented is from 1960 to current.

Artists Space

Address: 38 Greene Street (between Broome and Grand)
Open: Tuesday through Saturday, 10:00 am to 6:00 pm. Closed month of August and December 25th to January 1st.
Phone: (212) 226-3970
Comments: Gallery dedicated to showing seldom exhibited artists. Exhibitions, video and performance art are frequent, and shows are varied.

Arts for the Living Center of the Henry Street Settlement

Address: 466 Grand Street (between Pitt and Willet Streets)
Open: Tuesday through Saturday, Noon to 6:00 pm
Phone: (212) 598-0400
Comments: A Lower East Side arts center focused on promoting emerging artists. Hosts art shows of artists from the area.

Ceres

Address: 584 Broadway
Phone: (212) 226-4725
Comments: Dedicated to showing art primarily by women. The gallery is run by a women's cooperative.

Drawing Center, The

Address: 35 Wooster Street
Open: Tuesday, Thursday, Friday, 10:00 am to 6:00 pm; Wednesday, 10:00 am to 8:00 pm; Saturday, 11:00 am to 6:00 pm
Phone: (212) 219-2166
Comments: Devoted to showing works of drawing exclusively, The Drawing Center shows at least one historical exhibition a year, with the rest focusing on emerging or under-recognized and established contemporary artists in three to four "Selections" exhibitions annually.

Duggal Downtown Gallery

Address: 560 Broadway
Open: Monday through Friday, 8:30 am to 9:00 pm; Saturday, 8:30 am to 6:00 pm
Phone: (212) 941-7000
Comments: Shows photo exhibitions of innovative work on a regular basis.

Eleanor Ettinger Gallery

Address: 119 Spring Street
Open: Monday through Friday, 10:00 am to 6:00 pm; Saturday, 11:00 am to 6:00 pm; Sunday, Noon to 6:00 pm
Phone: (212) 925-7474
Comments: Ettinger's mandate is to find talented contemporary artists inspired by traditional schools, and it succeeds brilliantly. Artists it represents demonstrate technical mastery applied to contemporary themes and composition. Represented artists include Malcolm T. Liepke and David Hopkins.

Franklin Furnace

Address: New gallery location yet to be announced. Use Internet as temporary location: www.franklinfurnace.org.
Open: Tuesday through Saturday, Noon to 6:00 pm
Phone: (212) 925- 4671
Comments: A unique flagship for the alternative, this archive/gallery focuses on book art. Exhibits thousands of examples of modern books, pamphlets and other printed material designed by artists. At the time of printing this book, the gallery was preparing to create an electronic database of thousands of images capturing the work of artists in the last 20 years. This database is intended to be shown on its internet site. Call for latest information.

Fulcrum Gallery So-Soho

Address: 480 Broome Street
Open: Tuesday through Saturday, 11:00 am to 6:00 pm; Sunday, 1:00 pm to 6:00 pm
Phone: (212) 966-6848
Comments: Dedicated to showing emerging artists in painting and sculpture. Much of the work shown is abstract and "cutting edge."

Gagosian

Address: 136 Wooster Street (between Houston & Prince Streets)
Open: Tuesday through Saturday, 10:00 am to 6:00 pm
Phone: (212) 228-2828
Comments: The downtown counterpart to Gagosian's uptown flagship gallery, Gagosian specializes in contempory art, mostly sculpture.

Gallery Henoch

Address: 80 Wooster Street
Open: Tuesday through Saturday, 10:30 am to 6:00 pm
Phone: (212) 966-0303
Comments: Representing some 20 artists around the world, the sizable Henoch gallery is dedicated to realistic, contemporary painting and sculpture. It organizes about eight shows a year.

Gallery of Visual Arts, The

Address: 137 Wooster Street
Phone: (212) 598-0221
Comments: Exhibits artwork created by students at the School of Visual Arts, which runs the gallery.

Heller Gallery

Address: 71 Greene Street
Open: Tuesday through Saturday, 11:00 am to 6:00 pm
Phone: (212) 966-5948
Comments: One of the city's few galleries devoted solely to art glass, Heller holds about one show monthly, usually focusing on one glass blower, but sometimes has group shows. Has represented artists internationally since it opened in Soho in 1980.

Holly Solomon Gallery

Address: 172 Mercer Street, at Houston Street
Open: Tuesday through Friday, 10:00 am to 6:00 pm
Phone: (212) 941-5777
Comments: Specializes in contemporary art — about a dozen shows annually, including paintings and photographs.

Kenkeleba Gallery

Address: 214 East 2nd Street (between Avenues B and C)
Open: Tuesday through Saturday, 11:00 am to 6:00 pm, by appointment

Phone: (212) 674-3939
Comments: Specializing in African and Asian art, this gallery holds changing exhibitions, like "Transforming The Crown," which highlighted art works of African, Caribbean and Asian artists in the U.K. in the last thirty years.

Leo Castelli

Address: 420 West Broadway (between Spring & Prince Streets)
Open: Tuesday through Saturday, 10:00 am to 6:00 pm
Phone: (212) 431-5160
Comments: One of the most well-known galleries in the city, Castelli is distinguished by its strong roster of important contemporary artists it has represented over the last four decades. About eight shows a year.

Mimi Fertz Gallery

Address: 114 Prince Street
Open: Daily, 10:00 am to 6:00 pm; Saturday, 11:00 am to 7:00 pm
Phone: (212) 343-9377
Comments: Mimi Fertz Gallery specializes in Russian artists, many of whom were important dissidents who left the former Soviet Union before Glasnost. Some include: Mihail Chemiakin, Dmitri Plavinsky and Oscar Rabine. The gallery usually holds one-person shows during the winter, and group exhibitions in the summer months, and sponsors Russian cultural events, as well.

Perry Art Gallery

Address: 472 Broome Street
Open: Monday through Friday, 10:00 am to 6:00 pm; Saturday, 11:00 am to 6:00 pm; Sunday, Noon to 6:00 pm
Phone: (212) 925-6796
Comments: Perry specializes in 19th and 20th century posters, mostly used for advertising products and events, like films and festivals. Most are French, Spanish and Italian. Offers a glimpse into the history of commercial art design.

Pratt Manhattan

Address: 295 Lafayette Street, 2nd floor
Open: Monday through Saturday, 10:00 am to 6:00 pm
Phone: (212) 925-8481 (general number)
Comments: Exhibits works by Pratt students and faculty, representing an eclectic range of styles and media.

Sculptors Guild

Address: 110 Greene Street
Open: Tuesday and Thursday, 10:00 am to 5:00 pm
Phone: (212) 431-5669
Comments: The Sculptors Guild provides a forum for sculptors of nearly all media and styles, from emerging to veteran artists.

S.E. Feinman Fine Arts

Address: 448 Broome Street
Open: Monday through Saturday, 11:00 am to 5:45 pm; Sunday, Noon to 5:45 pm
Phone: (212) 431-6820
Comments: Represents some of the most distinguished contemporary print makers, as well as some talented young painters.

Witkin Gallery

Address: 415 West Broadway (at Spring Street)
Open: Tuesday through Friday, 11:00 am to 6:00 pm; Saturday, 11:00 am to 5:00 pm
Phone: (212) 925-5510
Comments: Has specialized in photographs by U.S. and international artists, including shows of work by Mario Cravo Neto and Margaret Courtney-Cooke.

World Financial Center Arts & Events Program

Address: On Hudson River at north end of Liberty Street
Phone: (212) 945-2600
Comments: Frequent exhibitions and installations are shown in the Courtyard Gallery, the North Bridge and the Liberty Street Gallery, all public spaces. Call for current shows.

Uptown

Antiquarium, Ltd.

Address: 948 Madison Avenue
Open: Tuesday through Friday, 10:00 am to 5:30 pm; Saturday, 11:00 am to 5:00 pm
Phone: (212) 734-9776
Comments: While Antiquarium is more a shop than a gallery, its uniqueness merits its inclusion in this chapter. On sale are Greek, Etruscan, Egyptian, Islamic and Roman antiquities including gold jewelry and

accessories as well as decorative objects and even a sarcophagus. Prices are understandably high.

Arsenal Gallery

Address: Fifth Avenue at 64th Street
Open: Monday through Friday, 9:30 am to 4:30 pm
Phone: (212) 360-8173
Comments: Housed in The Arsenal, a former munitions fortress that is now controlled by the Parks, Recreation and Cultural Affairs Department, the gallery hosts changing shows, which often center on Central Park.

Asia Society

Address: 725 Park Avenue (at 70th Street)
Open: Tuesday, Wednesday, Friday and Saturday, 10:00 am to 6:00 pm; Thursday, 11:00 am to 8:00 pm; Sunday, Noon to 5:00 pm. Free on Thursdays, 6:00 pm to 8:00 pm
Phone: Events information: (212) 517-NEWS; General information: (212) 288-6400
Comments: Hosts a fine program with changing exhibitions, including lectures, musical dance performances (most fee-based), related to Asian history and culture. However, the Society does open its doors free to the public on Thursdays, 6:00 pm to 8:00 pm. A recent exhibition was "Mandala: The Architecture of Enlightenment."

Bonni Benrubi

Address: 52 East 72nd Street
Open: Tuesday through Saturday, 11:00 am to 6:00 pm
Phone: (212) 517-3766
Comments: Known for its fine collection of 20th century photographs, with shows that have included Weegee, Robert Frank and Robert Evans.

China Institute Gallery

Address: 125 East 65th Street (between Lexington and Park Avenues)
Open: Monday, Wednesday and Saturday, 10:00 am to 5:00 pm; Tuesday, 10:00 am to 8:00 pm; Sunday, 1:00 pm to 5:00 pm
Phone: (212) 744-8181
Comments: A vibrant gallery with impressive exhibitions of work by Chinese and Chinese-American artists, the Gallery is run by the China Institute. A recent exhibition was "Power & Virtue: Horses in Chinese Art."

Cohen Gallery

Address: 1018 Madison Avenue (at 79th Street)
Open: Tuesday through Friday, 10:00 am to 6:00 pm
Phone: (212) 628-0303
Comments: An established seller of 20th century masters, including Chagall, Matisse, Miro and Warhol. Gallery is located on the 4th floor.

Dahesh Gallery

Address: 601 Fifth Avenue (at 48th Street)
Open: Tuesday through Saturday, 11:00 am to 6:00 pm
Phone: (212) 759-0606
Comments: Named after a Lebanese writer and art enthusiast, this museum/gallery offers 19th and 20th century paintings collected by Dahesh. Past shows included "Religion and the Rustic Image in Late Academic Art," paintings by 19th century French landscape and religious painters.

Equitable Gallery

Address: 787 Seventh Avenue (between 51st and 52nd Streets)
Phone: (212) 554-4818
Comments: A prominent Upper West Side gallery featuring compelling shows, which recently included, "Arts of Africa, Oceania, and the Americas from the Raymond and Laura Wielgus Collection," showing Pre-Columbian artifacts and ceramics.

Forbes Magazine Galleries

Address: 62 Fifth Avenue (near 12th Street)
Open: Thursday is reserved for group tours. Tuesday, Wednesday, Friday and Saturday, 10:00 am to 4:00 pm
Phone: (212) 206-5548
Comments: Publisher Malcolm Forbes' showcase of his collections, ranging from Faberge Easter eggs and jewels to the Presidential Papers, an array of documents revealing aspects of American Presidents' lives.

Foundation For Hellenic Culture

Address: 7 West 57th Street
Phone: (212) 308-6908
Comments: Dedicated to promoting Greek language, culture and art, the Foundation offers free art exhibitions and lectures as part of its program. Events are found on web site: http://www.hri.org/fhc.

Gagosian

Address: 980 Madison Avenue (at 76th Street)
Open: Winter: Tuesday through Saturday, 10:00 am to 6:00 pm; Summer: Monday through Friday, 10:00 am to 6:00 pm
Phone: (212) 744-2313
Comments: Gagosian focuses on contemporary painting in its generous exhibition space.

Godel & Co.

Address: 39A East 72nd Street
Open: Monday through Friday, 10:00 am to 6:00 pm; Saturday, 10:00 am to 5:00 pm
Phone: (212) 288-7272
Comments: Specializing in 19th and 20th century fine art, Godel holds three to four exhibitions yearly. Included in its collection are classics on American painting, including Frederic Church and James Whistler.

Grolier Club, The

Address: 47 East 60th Street
Open: Exhibitions held from October through June. Monday through Saturday, 10:00 am to 5:00 pm
Phone: (212) 838-6690
Comments: The Club focuses on the craft of bookmaking, and houses exhibitions on books, prints and manuscripts, and other related topics from October through June.

HAF

Address: 79 Grand Street
Open: Tuesday through Saturday, 11:00 am to 7:00 pm
Phone: (212) 925-3100
Comments: One of the very few furniture design galleries, this Soho establishment showcases the work of one artist: Hassan Abouseda. Included in his porfolio are slick, but utilitarian glass and fine wood tables, chairs and bedroom furniture.

Hammer Gallery

Address: 33 West 57th Street
Open: Monday through Friday, 9:30 am to 5:30 pm; Saturday, 10:00 am to 5:00 pm
Phone: (212) 644-4405
Comments: Hammer Gallery focuses on American and European, 19th

and 20th century paintings. In addition, at its Hammer Graphics, housed in the same gallery, it sells original watercolors, paintings and pastels by LeRoy Nieman.

Hirsch & Adler Galleries

Address: 21 East 70th Street (at Madison Avenue)
Open: Tuesday through Friday, 9:30 am to 5:30 pm
Phone: (212) 535-8810
Comments: Hirsch & Adler should satisfy all tastes: on the ground floor it offers fine paintings through the centuries; upstairs, it has devoted to its impressive modern collection, which includes classics and its own gallery artists.

International Center of Photography

Address: 1130 East 94th Street (at Fifth Avenue)
Open: Tuesday, Noon to 8:00 pm; Wednesday though Sunday, Noon to 6:00 pm. Voluntary contribution Tuesday, 6:00 pm to 8:00 pm
Phone: (212) 768-4680
Comments: Intended use is for members, but this photography hub does offer exhibitions and lectures on photography, and is open on a voluntary admission fee basis on Tuesday, 5:00 pm to 8:00 pm. Also visit the midtown branch at 1133 Avenue of the Americas at 43rd Street (212) 768-4682.

James Graham & Sons

Address: 1014 Madison Avenue (at 78th Street)
Open: Tuesday through Saturday, 9:30 am to 5:30 pm
Phone: (212) 535-5767
Comments: Established in 1857, James Graham & Sons is billed as the oldest family-run art gallery in New York. It represents estates of important American 19th and 20th century painters. It also has an impressive collection of sculpture in its basement gallery.

Kennedy

Address: 730 Fifth Avenue (at 56th and 57th Streets)
Open: Tuesday through Saturday, 9:30 am to 5:30 pm
Phone: (212) 541-9600
Comments: Kennedy's collection includes a broad range of American painting from the 18th century to contemporary. Represented are: Eakins, Peale and Whistler.

Kenneth W. Rendell Gallery

Address: 989 Madison Avenue (between 76th and 77th Streets)
Open. Monday through Saturday, 10:00 am to 6:00 pm
Phone: (212) 717-1776
Comments: The Rendell Gallery specializes in rare historical letters and documents, ranging from Thomas Jefferson to Duke Ellington. The gallery has the precious airs of a university rare book room.

Korean Cultural Service

Address: 460 Park Avenue (at 57th Street)
Open: Monday through Friday, 10:00 am to 4:30 pm
Phone: (212) 759-9550; (212) 593-0742
Comments: Offers changing art shows by Korean as well as non-Korean artists, featuring knot decorative arts, painting, sculpture.

Kouros

Address: 23 East 73rd Street
Open: Tuesday through Saturday, 10:30 am to 6:00 pm
Phone: (212) 288-5888
Comments: Kouros offers an eclectic collection of contemporary and modern paintings, but its forte lies in sculpture — big and diminuative, abstract and figurative.

Langham Leff Gallery

Address: 19 East 71st Street
Open: Monday through Friday, 11:00 am to 6:00 pm; Saturday, 11:00 am to 5:00 pm
Phone: (212) 288-4030
Comments: Langham Leff distinguishes itself with a cornucopia of rare object d'art, paintings, furniture, and accessories, mostly from the 16th to 20th centuries and from all over the world. The collection is the result of years of careful selection, lending the gallery a museum feel.

Leonard Hutton

Address: 41 East 57th Street
Open: Tuesday through Saturday, 10:00 am to 5:30 pm
Phone: (212) 751-7373
Comments: Specializes in 20th century and contemporary European masters, including Kandinsky, Miro, Picasso, and Klee.

M. Knoedler & Co Inc

Address: 19 East 70th Street (between Madison & Fifth Avenues)
Open: Tuesday through Friday, 9:30 am to 5:30 pm; Saturday, 10:00 am to 5:30 pm
Phone: (212) 794-0550
Comments: Knoedler, established in 1846, is one of the nation's oldest art galleries and has sold works to some of this country's most important collectors and art institutions. Today, it serves as the agent for a roster of estates that includes some of the masters of this century: Frank Stella, Robert Motherwell, and Adolph Gottlieb.

Marlborough

Address: 40 West 57th Street (between Fifth & Sixth Avenues)
Open: Monday through Saturday, 10:00 am to 5:30 pm
Phone: (212) 541-4900
Comments: Marlborough focuses on modern art (from around 1940 to the present) by American, British and Latin American artists. Most of the collection is realistic and pop art, and the media represented include paintings, sculpture, drawings and prints.

Miram and Ira D. Wallach Art Gallery, Columbia University

Address: Schmerhorn Hall, Columbia University, Broadway at 116th Street
Phone: (212) 854-1754
Comments: An impressive university art gallery with compelling exhibitions. Past exhibitions included: "Apostles in England: Sir James Thornhill and the Legacy of Raphael's Tapestry Cartoons." Adjunct to art history department, with shows having a scholarly bent.

PaceWildenstein

Address: 32 East 57th Street (between Park & Madison Avenues)
Open: Tuesday through Friday, 9:30 am to 6:00 pm
Phone: (212) 421-3292
Comments: One of the city's hallmarks for contemporary art, with its four floors dedicated to paintings, sculpture and photography. Pace Prints, with an emphasis on photography, is housed on its own floor. Routinely shows changing exhibitions of prominent artists. Call ahead, because hours vary throughout the year.

Paine Webber Art Gallery

Address: 1285 Sixth Avenue (between 51st and 52nd Streets)
Open: Monday through Friday, 8:00 am to 6:00 pm
Phone: (212) 713-2885
Comments: Collaborates with other large institutions to show about a half dozen exhibitions per year on a wide range of themes. Call to find out the current or upcoming show.

Sculpture Center

Address: 167 East 69th Street (between Third & Lexington Avenues)
Open: Tuesday through Saturday, 11:00 am to 5:00 pm. Closed July, August
Phone: (212) 879-3500
Comments: The Center sponsors roughly a half dozen shows a year, focusing on sculpture, and is one of the few galleries of its kind in the city. A recent show was entitled, "Suspended Instants," which showcased work by New York and Rio de Janeiro artists.

Society of Illustrators

Address: 128 East 63rd Street (at Lexington Avenue)
Open: Tuesday, 10:00 am to 8:00 pm; Wednesday through Friday, 10:00 am to 5:00 pm; Saturday, Noon to 4:00 pm
Phone: (212) 838-2560
Comments: Houses changing exhibitions in its two galleries, mostly on commercial art — many of which have become entrenched in our contemporary life — done by artists well regarded outside the advertising realm, such as Norman Rockwell. The society's permanent collection, which numbers over 2,000 pieces, is also represented by a few hundred selections on display.

Taipei Gallery

Address: 1230 Avenue of the Americas
Phone: (212) 373-1800
Comments: Operated by the Chinese Information and Cultural Center, this gallery offers changing exhibitions on contemporary and traditional Chinese and other Asian art. Recent shows included "Asian Traditions: Modern Expressions," a survey of Asian American artists from 1945 to 1970.

Wildenstein

Address: 19 East 64th Street
Open: Monday through Saturday, 10:00 am to 5:00 pm
Phone: (212) 879-0500
Comments: A palatial townhouse welcomes visitors at Wildenstein, which specializes in traditional and classical painting, sculpture and drawings. Possesses a clubby, museum feel.

Gardens

New York has some well-appreciated greenery in its elegant gardens throughout the boroughs. Some of the gardens listed in this chapter are known nationally for their breadth of rare plantings and the intense work committed to keeping the environment healthy and well-maintained. They offer transporting experiences for the bedraggled New Yorker tired of asphalt and traffic jams.

Alley Pond Environmental Center

Address: 228-06 Northern Boulevard, Douglastown, Queens
Open: Monday through Saturday, 9:00 am to 4:30 pm; Sunday, 9:30 am to 3:30 pm (except July and August)
Phone: (718) 229-4000
Comments: Including some 150 acres of wetlands, this center serves primarily as an educational center. It has trails for children as well as an aquarium and a small animal room.

Brooklyn Botanic Garden

Address: 1000 Washington Street (at Prospect Park), Brooklyn
Open: Hours vary throughout year, but open usually during daylight hours. Closed on Mondays.
Phone: (718) 622-4433
Comments: One of Brooklyn's gems, replete with thousands of plantings, including a rose garden, greenhouse with tropical plants, and a Japanese theme garden. While a nominal fee is charged during the summer months, it is free on Tuesdays throughout the year and weekdays during the winter. Also hosts lectures and horticultural programs, plant sales, etc.

Cloisters, The

Address: Fort Tyrone Park, Washington Heights
Open: Tuesday through Sunday, 9:30 am to 4:45 pm
Phone: (212) 923-3700
Comments: An impressive reconstruction of European Gothic and medieval architectural remnants combined to produce a sprawling monastery-like edifice. Houses much of the Metropolitan Museum of Art's medieval collection including tapestries, altars, panels and illuminated manuscripts. While there is a suggested admission charge to visit inside the cloisters, the gardens outside are one of the most romantic

spots in the city — and can be visited for free.

High Rock Conservation Center, The
Address: 200 Nevada Avenue, Staten Island
Open: Daily, 9:00 am to 5:00 pm
Comments: A 90-odd acre forested refuge with pockets of water and swamplands. Also has a Young Naturalist Program, and a garden for blind visitors.

New York Botanical Garden
Address: 200th Street at Southern Boulevard
Open: November through March, 10:00 am to 4:00 pm; April through October, 9:00 am to 6:00 pm
Phone: (718) 817-8700
Comments: One of New York's most beautiful places, the Botanical Garden comprises some 250 acres including a conservatory with 11 glass pavilions and various gardens devoted to specific themes (e.g., the Chemurgic Garden, Rock and Native Plant Gardens; Perennial Garden, Lilac Collection; and the Forest.) Also on the premises is the Snuff Mill, built by tobacco businessman Pierre Lorillard. Free only on Wednesday and Saturday, 10:00 am to noon.

Queens Botanical Garden
Address: 43-50 Main Street at Dahlia Street, Flushing, Queens
Phone: (718) 886-3800
Comments: A sprawling oasis with countless rare plantings and trails. Also home to many cultural events, workshops, and educational programs. In the past, hosted "Up, Up and Away," a workshop aimed at teaching the fundamentals of aerodynamics through the building and flying of kites.

Socrates Sculpture Park
Address: 31-29 Vernon Boulevard, Long Island City, Queens.
Open: Summer hours: 10:00 am to dusk; Winter hours: Saturday and Sunday only, 10:00 am to dusk
Phone: (718) 956-1819
Comments: Built on an old marine terminal, the garden is a good example of revived urban wasteland. It is home to changing exhibitions of new artists.

United Nations Garden

Address: First Avenue at 45th Street
Comments: A popular large garden near the UN, and the East River.

Wave Hill Center for Environmental Studies

Address: 675 West 252nd Street
Open: Open every day, 10:00 am to 4:30 pm. After Memorial Day, hours are extended to 5:30 pm, Wednesday until dark, and on Sunday until 7:00 pm. Free only on weekdays.
Phone: (718) 549-2055
Comments: Once a sprawling estate perched on the banks of the Hudson River, Wave Hill was donated to the city in 1960 and is now devoted to environmental studies. The Center holds exhibitions and concerts, and has an extensive collection of plants housed in greenhouses and on the grounds. In the past, workshops included "Botanical Printing," and "Design a Bouquet for Mother's Day."

Gay/Lesbian

Myriad organizations and local groups serve New York's large homosexual community. This list focuses on some of the more established groups devoted to serving gays and lesbians through workshops, legal defense as well as social events. Most should, however, be used as places for advice and referrals first, and free events second.

GLAAD-NY (Gay and Lesbian Alliance)
Address: 150 West 26th Street (at Seventh Avenue), Suite 503
Phone: (212) 807-1700
Comments: A watchdog group tracking the media's treatment of gays and lesbians. Hosts talks on these topics.

Identity House
Address: 39 West 14th Street (between Fifth and Sixth Avenues), Suite 205
Phone: (212) 243-8181
Comments: Opened in 1971, Identity House offers free peer counseling and referrals for single sex couples and single lesbians and gays. Also offers "come out" groups and a "discussion series." Call for times.

Lamda Legal Defense and Education Fund
Address: 666 Broadway, 12th floor
Phone: (212) 809-8585
Comments: LAMDA sponsors some services and events free of charge, but its primary mandate is to combat discrimination against gays and lesbians. Accepts requests for advice on discrimination cases on Monday, Wednesday and Friday, 2:00 pm to 4:00 pm.

Lesbian and Gay Community Services Center
Address: 208 West 13th Street
Phone: (212) 620-7310
Comments: A vibrant center for information for the lesbian and gay community and all those interested in it, this Center is a sort of umbrella organization for many organizations providing all types of

events, including lectures, performances, counseling groups, etc.

New York Area Bisexual Network

Phone: (212) 459-4784
Comments: A central clearinghouse phone contact for information on events and services for support groups and various events for gays and lesbians. Call for recorded message detailing group meetings, times and locations.

Shades of Lavender

Address: 470 Bergen Street (at Flatbush Avenue), Brooklyn
Phone: (718) 622-2910
Comments: Support group dedicated to serving the interests of the gay and lesbian community.

Happy Hours (with free appetizers)

Getting a drink and an appetizer at a bar in New York can run up to $20 at some places, making a quick stop to a watering hole an unexpectedly expensive affair. But when half-price drinks and free shrimp cocktail are added to the equation, suddenly things get happier. Listed here are a selected few of the outstanding Happy Hours which include discounted drinks, respectable chicken wings to embarrassingly lavish free hors d'oeuvres and pleasant surroundings. Of course, the free food is served to draw business during normally sluggish hours at bars, so few would discourage turning offered snacks into a light dinner.

If you have the chance, do call ahead to ensure that these Happy Hours are still being offered: the level of generosity at restaurants and bars routinely slides (both for the better or for the worse). This is by no means a complete list, but rather highlights spots which are known for dependable Happy Hours.

Alamo
Address: 304 East 48th Street
Phone: (212) 759-0590
Comments: This Tex-Mex bar/restaurant serves up Mexican specialties during its Happy Hour held on weekdays from 5:00 pm to 7:00 pm.

Cecil's Bar, Crown Plaza Hotel at the United Nations
Address: 304 East 42nd Street (between First and Second Avenues)
Phone: (212) 297-3456
Comments: Complimentary hors d'oeuvres at this swanky U.N. hangout.

Donald Sachs
Address: 220 Vesey Street
Phone: (212) 619-4600
Comments: A standard for Wall Street commuters, this World Financial Center establishment offers up free food with drinks during its Happy Hour on Tuesdays from 3:00 pm to 8:00 pm.

Eamon Doran

Address: 174 Montague Street, Brooklyn Heights
Phone: (718) 596-4969
Comments: Daily Happy Hour including free bar food (wings and raw vegetables) at this popular Brooklyn Heights Irish Pub.

Harry's Bar, the New York Helmsley

Address: 212 East 42nd Street (between Second and Third Avenues)
Phone: (212) 490-8900
Comments: Serves up shrimp and other free appetizers at the bar, plus piano music in late afternoons for no cover or drink minimum.

Montague Street Saloon

Address: 122 Montague Street, Brooklyn Heights
Phone: (718) 522-6770
Comments: A popular Brooklyn Heights destination, this saloon serves rounds of free appetizers after 5:00 pm until around 7:30 pm for its Happy Hours, which are held Monday through Friday.

Players Sports Bar, The New York Hilton and Towers

Address: 111 West 53rd Street (between Sixth and Seventh Avenues)
Phone: (212) 261-5896
Comments: Free buffet on weekdays in this popular sports bar, which also has its share of TV screens and an assortment of games as well.

Senor Swanky's

Address: 287 Columbus Avenue (at 73rd Street)
Phone: (212) 501-7000
Comments: This restaurant/bar offers food during its Happy Hours in the bar Monday through Friday, from 4:00 pm to 7:00 pm.

Tatou

Address: 151 East 50th Street (between Lexington and Third)
Phone: (212) 753-1144
Comments: Tatou offers complimentary hors d'oeuvres on weekdays during its Happy Hour, which begins around 5:30 pm.

T.G. Whitney's

Address: 244 East 53rd Street

Phone: (212) 888-5772

Comments: Free Buffalo-style chicken wings every night from 5:00 pm to 7:00 pm during the Happy Hour at this Upper East Side pub.

Health Services

Most selections in this chapter are useful as clearinghouses for information, referrals, outreach hotlines, lectures and workshops. Some offer these services for all, but are primarily dedicated to serving the especially needy or indigent. Unless you fall into that category, it would be inappropriate to accept those services.

These organizations generally aim to augment services already provided under one's health coverage, with an emphasis on cancer detection, HIV testing and psychological counseling. This list is by no means complete, but should serve as a solid first step for people looking for information and help on a number of the most common illnesses and disorders.

Alianza Dominicana
Address: 715 West 179th Street
Phone: (212) 795-4226
Comments: Based in Washington Heights, this group offers free anonymous HIV blood and oral testing. Tests administered Monday, 10:00 am to 6:00 pm; Wednesday, Noon to 8:00 pm.

American Anorexia/Bulimia Association
Address: 165 West 46th Street, Suite 1108
Phone: (212) 575-6200
Comments: Offers free support group meetings and a wealth of information, community outreach and referral services. Provides assistance to sufferers of bulimia and anorexia, as well as to people close to them. Also provides a wealth of information on other national organizations and private groups.

American Menopause Foundation, Inc.
Address: The Empire State Building, 350 Fifth Avenue, Suite 2822
Phone: (212) 714-2398
Comments: This not-for-profit organization offers help and advice on menopause issues through support groups and referrals. Serves individuals as well as companies. Founded in 1993, the foundation is the nation's only not-for-profit health organization dedicated solely to providing support and assistance on issues concerning menopause.

Bellevue Hospital Center

Address: 462 First Avenue (at 17th Street and First Avenue)
Phone: (212) 562-3291
Comments: Provides walk-in clinic care for cancer screening and assistance with getting care and treatment. Charge is free to sliding scale. Screening nurse on duty from 8:30 am to 2:00 pm, Monday through Friday.

BRC Human Services Corp.

Address: 191 Chrystie Street
Open: Monday through Friday, 9:00 am to 2:00 pm
Phone: (212) 533-5151
Comments: Aimed at the indigent elderly population, this private, non-profit organization provides free cancer prevention, screening and detection services for most common cancers. Doctors are in Tuesdays and Thursdays.

Breast Examination Center of Harlem

Address: Harlem State Office Building, 163 West 125th Street, 4th floor
Open: Monday through Friday, 8:30 am to 4:00 pm
Phone: (212) 864-0600
Comments: Offers free screenings for detection of breast and cervical cancer as well as support groups for those who have undergone breast cancer surgery.

Breast Examination Center of Harlem

Address: 163 West 125th Street, State Office Building, 4th floor
Open: 9:00 am to 5:00 pm, Monday through Friday
Phone: (212) 864-0600
Comments: Free screening facility for detection of breast cancer, also offering workshops, seminars, conferences and support groups.

Bureau of Maternity Services and Family Planning, New York City Department of Health

Address: 2 Lafayette Street
Phone: (212) 442-1740
Comments: This agency is mostly geared to aiding and educating low-income, teen-age women, but is naturally eager to assist all other women. Provides a wealth of information on reproductive health, including its Women's Healthline — (212) 230 -1111 — free pregnancy tests, fam-

ily planning, counseling and health education workshops. Also offers referral services.

Cancer Information Service (CIS)

Phone: 1-800-4-CANCER

Comments: The CIS offers an information line for cancer programs and services located across the country. The service helps callers understand, in simple language, latest scientific information pertaining to cancer. Callers will be able to find out what low cost or free cancer screening tests (e.g., breast, skin, prostrate) are available in the metropolitan area. The web site is also very helpful (http://rex.nci.nih.gov). Bear in mind, low-cost and free screenings are generally intended for the indigent population and/or those uncovered by insurance.

Columbia Presbyterian Center for Women's Health

Phone: (800) 227-CPMC

Comments: Columbia Presbyterian offers a hotline number for free referrals and services as a sort of clearinghouse for information on women's health issues.

Community Family Planning Council

Phone: (800) 955-2372

Comments: Offers free HIV tests at its eight sites plus mobile units.

David Geffen Center for HIV Prevention and Health Education

Phone: (212) 367-1100

Comments: Based in Chelsea, this center offers confidential HIV screening tests. Free referrals, and free counseling.

Gilda's Club

Address: 195 West Houston Street

Phone: (212) 647-9700

Comments: A free, non-profit support group for people with cancer, as well as their friends and family. Named after SNL comedienne Gilda Radner, the group also offers support services, workshops and lectures.

Harlem Hospital Saturday Morning Screening

Address: 506 Lenox Avenue
Phone: (212) 939-1470
Comments: Offers free PAP, breast, rectal, cervical exams on Saturdays, 10:00 am to 11:45 am. Clinic hours are Thursday, 1:00 pm to 3:45 pm.

Health Education Center

Address: 1080 Lexington Avenue
Phone: (212) 439-2980
Comments: Provides free screenings, and scores of free booklets on conditions and illnesses.

Montifiore Medical Center

Phone: (for ages 13 to 21): (718) 881-TEST; (over age 21): (718) 920-6752
Comments: A Bronx-based service offering oral HIV testing for those 13 years old and up.

National Alliance of Breast Cancer Organizations (NABCO)

Address: 9 East 37th Street, 10th floor
Phone: (212) 889-0606
Comments: NABCO is a network of breast cancer groups dedicated to assisting and giving referrals. Also has a helpful web site (www.nabco.org).

New York City Department of Health

Phone: (800) TALK-HIV
Comments: Held at 12 sites throughout the city, provides free, anonymous HIV blood screening.

Positive Health Project

Address: 301 West 37th Street (between Eighth and Ninth Avenues)
Phone: (212) 465-8305
Comments: A mid-town HIV blood testing center free of charge, held on Wednesdays, 2:30 pm to 4:30 pm.

SHARE: Self-Help for Women with Breast or Ovarian Cancer

Address: 1510 Broadway, Suite 1720
Phone: (212) 719-0364
Comments: Offers support to women with breast or ovarian cancer who need help coping socially and psychologically, through a hotline, support groups and various educational programs, all free of charge.

Women's Health Forum

Address: CUNY Graduate Center, 33 West 42nd Street (between Fifth and Sixth Avenues)
Phone: (212) 642-1600
Comments: Sponsors free lectures, assistance and panel discussions on women's health issues.

Jazz, Rock & Folk Music

It seems there is little logic to why some bars and clubs charge a $10 cover for an ordinary band and demand you buy at least two drinks and others welcome you in for free and let you drink only when you're thirsty. Sometimes it's because you get what you pay for, but not all the time. The selection in this chapter includes those places which regularly offer good to great live music without cover charge. Almost none require a minimum drink purchase.

The range of music encountered in the spots highlighted here is enormous: punk, jazz, hip hop, folk, garage band, traditional Irish, etc. Some may be stiff and formal; others may smell of the beer served the night before. Naturally, these places are usually standing room on Friday and Saturday nights, but during the week it's tamer. Note that some listings do not have hours, mainly because they vary; but in most cases, starting times for sets are mentioned.

alt.coffee
Address: 139 Avenue A
Phone: (212) 529-2233
Comments: A popular, low-key East Village café featuring live bands, cover-free.

Arlene Grocery
Address: 95 Stanton Street
Open: Daily, 6:00 pm to 2:00 am
Phone: (212) 358-1633
Comments: Very popular no cover, no drink minimum bar with live bands almost nightly.

Arthur's Tavern
Address: 57 Grove Street
Open: Sunday and Monday, 8:00 pm to 4:00 am; Tuesday through Saturday, 7:00 pm to 4:00 am
Phone: (212) 675-6879
Comments: Free live jazz every night at this landmark Greenwich Village club. Music often spills over into the early morning hours.

Bell Caffe

Address: 310 Spring Street
Phone: (212) 334-2355
Comments: Music nightly at this relaxed coffee house/restaurant, with unpredictable types of bands and performers. $7 drink minimum. Mostly jazz, but sitar on Tuesdays.

Centerfold Coffeehouse at the Church of St. Paul

Address: West End Avenue (at 86th Street)
Phone: (212) 866-4454
Comments: This offbeat church opens its doors to free performances and folk music and poetry readings, mostly on Fridays. Donations are suggested and assumed, but not required. Call for details on free events.

Ciel Rouge

Address: 176 Seventh Avenue (between 20th and 21st Streets)
Open: 7:00 pm to after midnight, daily.
Phone: (212) 929-5542
Comments: Unique Chelsea French-themed salon featuring torch songs and assorted low key jazz performances. No cover, no minimum.

Desmond's Tavern

Address: 433 Park Avenue South (at 29th Street)
Open: Sets begin around 9:30 pm
Phone: (212) 725-9864
Comments: Has a local bar atmosphere, features mostly rock bands Thursday through Saturday nights until around 4.00 am.

Detour

Address: 349 East 13th Street (at First Avenue)
Phone: (212) 533-6212
Comments: This East Village jazz club offers no cover, no drinks minimum jazz nightly beginning at 9:00 pm on weekdays and 9:30 on weekends.

Divine Bar

Address: 244 East 51st Street (between 2nd and 3rd Avenues)
Open: Monday through Friday, 5:00 pm to 2:30 am; Saturday and Sunday, 7:00 pm to 2:30 am
Phone: (212) 319-WINE
Comments: Popular, quiet East Side wine bar/lounge, offering live

acoustic music free of charge on Sundays, after 8:00 pm.

Don't Tell Mama

Address: 343 West 46th Street
Phone: (212) 757-0788
Comments: Jazz piano seven nights a week beginning at 9:00 pm along with singing waiters at this popular Broadway venue.

Druids

Address: 736 10th Avenue (near 50th Street)
Phone: (212) 307-6410
Comments: Usually light jazz (trios or a few horns) Saturdays and Mondays from around 10:00 pm to 2:00 am. No cover, no minimum.

Ear Inn

Address: 326 Spring Street
Phone: (212) 226-9060
Comments: With sets beginning at 11:00 pm usually Monday through Wednesday, this popular Soho area bar offers a smattering of bands, mostly focusing on blues. No cover.

Ed Sullivan's Restaurant

Address: 1697 Broadway (between 53rd and 54th Street)
Phone: (212) 541-1697
Comments: Live music with no cover at this small but popular eatery, located next to "Late Show with David Letterman." Bands usually straight-ahead or swing, with sets beginning at 8:00 pm on weekdays and 9:00 pm on weekends.

Elbow Room

Address: 144 Bleeker Street
Phone: (212) 979-8434
Comments: No cover jazz and piano at this relaxed Greenwich Village establishment.

Garage Restaurant & Cafe

Address: 99 Seventh Avenue South (off Grove Street)
Open: Monday through Saturday, Noon to 4:00 am; Brunch Saturday and Sunday, Noon to 4:00 pm
Phone: (212) 645-0600
Comments: This respected steakhouse offers free jazz to diners and

café dwellers each night and during brunch. Call for times and bands slated, for they do vary. Patrons are welcome to have a drink at the bar without charge for the music. Most nights, sets begin at 9:00 pm.

Grand Hyatt Hotel

Address: Park Avenue (at 42nd Street)
Phone: (212) 883-1234
Comments: Piano on weekend evenings until midnight with no drink minimum required in the elegant "Trumpets" restaurant/lounge at this high profile hotel near Grand Central Station.

Hotel Galvez

Address: 103 Avenue B (between Sixth and Seventh Streets)
Phone: (212) 358-9683
Comments: A full program of rock bands of varying quality, but almost always free.

Jules

Address: 65 St. Mark's Place (between First and Second Avenues)
Phone: (212) 477-5560
Comments: No cover, no minimum jazz, featuring trios and bands with strong African influences. During the week, sets are from 5:30 pm to 1:00 am and from 5:30 pm to 2:00 am on the weekends.

L'ecco Italia

Address: 289 Bleeker Street
Open: Monday through Thursday, Noon to 1:00 am; Friday and Saturday, Noon to 3:00 am; Sunday, Noon to 1:00 am
Phone: (212) 929-3355
Comments: Beginning at 8:00 pm every night, this popular jazz club/ restaurant features a no-cover piano bar, and other bands later in the evening.

La Table Des Rois

Address: 135 East 50th Street (between Third and Lexington Avenues)
Phone: (212) 838-7275
Comments: A pleasant, romantic spot for listening and dancing to Big Band and Swing music at this French restaurant/dance club on Wednesday, Friday and Saturdays. On Saturdays, free piano bar from 5:00 pm to 10:00 pm.

Lenox Lounge

Address: 288 Lenox Avenue (between 124th and 125th Street)
Phone: (212) 722-9566
Comments: No cover on Monday night, from midnight to 4:00 am at this popular spot known for its jazz and alternative music. Two drink minimum, some nights.

Ludlow Street Cafe

Address: 165 Ludlow Street
Phone: (212) 353-0536
Comments: Each night, one or more bands take to the stage in this popular spot for a youngish crowd on the increasingly trendy Lower East Side.

Manny's Car Wash

Address: 1558 Third Avenue
Phone: (212) 369-2583
Comments: No cover charge before 9:00 pm nightly at this Western/Blues joint.

Metronome

Address: 915 Broadway (at 21st Street)
Phone: (212) 505-7400
Comments: Trios and quartets from Thursday to Saturday from 8:00 pm to midnight. Two drink minimum.

Mitchell's Place

Address: 134 Reade Street
Phone: (212) 226-8928
Comments: This TriBeCa pub brings live jazz and blues bands on Friday nights, usually starting around 10:00 pm. No cover.

New School for Social Research, Jazz Division

Address: 55 West 13th Street, 5th floor
Phone: (212) 229-5896 ext. 305
Comments: From late November through December, the program offers free jazz concerts almost daily — mostly performed by students and faculty — through its "Ensemble & Recital Series." During the rest of the year, free concerts are scattered, and occur about twice monthly. Call for upcoming events or request calendar of events.

Ryan's Irish Pub
Address: 151 Second Avenue (between Ninth and Tenth Avenues)
Phone: (212) 979-9511
Comments: Open mike traditional Irish music every Sunday night at 9:00 pm at this authentic Irish pub.

Savoy Lounge
Address: 355 West 41st Street (between Eighth and Ninth Avenues)
Phone: (212) 947-5255
Comments: Live jazz, no cover on occasion, but usually the cover is about $3. Sets usually begin at 10:00 pm during the week. Focuses on traditional quartets and blues bands.

Sazerac House
Address: 533 Hudson Street
Open: Music begins: Friday and Saturday: 9:30 pm, 11:00 pm, and 12:30 am
Phone: (212) 989-0313
Comments: Welcomes those who wish to take a drink at the bar and listen — cover-free — to the jazz, usually playing during brunch on Sunday, noon to 3:00 pm.

Sophia's
Address: 221 West 46th Street
Phone: (212) 719-5799
Comments: Live jazz, no cover, no minimum, 7:00 pm to midnight from Tuesday to Saturday. Piano on Sundays and Mondays.

Swing 46
Address: 349 West 46th Street (between Eighth and Ninth Avenues)
Open: Daily, 5:00 pm to 2:00 am
Phone: (212) 262-9554
Comments: Live Swing music by big band each night, plus free dancing lessons every Tuesday, Wednesday and Thursday.

Teddy's Bar and Grill
Address: 96 Berry Street, Williamsburg, Brooklyn
Open: 11:00 am to early morning hours
Phone: (718) 384-9787
Comments: A wide assortment of bands — reggae to jazz, blues, folk and Latin — at this landmark turn-of-the-century Williamsburg res-

taurant and bar on Thursday and Saturday. No cover, no minimum.

Visiones

Address: 125 MacDougal Street
Phone: (212) 673-5576
Comments: Quickly becoming one of New York's hottest jazz clubs, lifts cover charges on some nights, so call ahead and find out when.

Zuni

Address: 598 Ninth Avenue (near 43rd Street)
Phone: (212) 765-7626
Comments: No cover, no minimum, jazz from 8:00 pm until midnight on Mondays. Usually a guitar, bass and sax trio.

Lectures

To limit a chapter on lectures to the few below is a bit misleading. Many more places for lectures can be found in the "Libraries", "Institutes and Societies", "Cultural Centers" and "Literary Events" chapters. Also, organizations and groups dedicated to any given interest (e.g., Women's Centers, The Skyscraper Museum) usually have lectures. Naturally, the City's universities offer many lectures to the public, as do museums.

New York is an especially vibrant center for speakers and attracts leaders in all fields of interest. The advantage of attending lectures often lies in the question and answer sessions typically following talks. Most lectures are organized into series, and are clustered during the academic year, so it's difficult to find places that have regular talks at a fixed time and place. Below are some places which are known especially for their lecture programs. Most lectures attract a serious audience, and demand a great deal of respect and attention.

Architectural League of New York, Urban Center
Address: 457 Madison Avenue (at 51st Street)
Phone: (212) 753-1722
Comments: Holds lectures on issues relating to urban design and architecture. Call for events open free to the public.

City University of New York
Address: Call or visit CUNY's Office of Community relations, 535 East 80th Street during office hours
Phone: (212) 794-5555
Comments: CUNY, with 21 campuses spread throughout the city, hosts myriad lectures and events open and free to the public.

Columbia University
Address: West 116th Street
Phone: (212) 854-1754
Comments: While Columbia hosts numerous lectures open and free to the public, there exists no useful clearinghouse to find these events, apart from The Record, an administration-run newspaper basically only

found on the campus. Departments sponsoring lectures and other events sporadically advertise to the outer-Columbia world. The best advice for finding lectures is to contact departments directly.

Cooper Union
Address: Third Avenue (at 7th Street)
Phone: (212) 353-4195
Comments: Hosts a rich variety of lectures from renowned writers and artists, many of which are free.

Jewish Theological Seminary
Address: 3080 Broadway (at 122nd Street)
Phone: (212) 678-8000
Comments: The Seminary is known for its full program of lectures, many free. Not all focus on Jewish issues and culture.

Municipal Art Society's Urban Center
Address: 457 Madison Avenue (between 50th and 51st Streets)
Open: Monday, Tuesday, Wednesday and Friday, 11:00 am to 5:00 pm
Phone: (212) 935-3960
Comments: Formed by the Municipal Art Society, a group established in 1893 to improve New York's state of public art, the Center is devoted to preserving and expanding the city's buildings and parks. Holds lectures and public events to this end. Also, offers a gallery with changing exhibitions related to its mission.

New Museum of Contemporary Art
Address: 583 Broadway
Open: Wednesday, noon to 6:00 pm; Thursday through Saturday, Noon to 8:00 pm; Sunday, Noon to 6:00 pm
Phone: (212) 219-1222
Comments: This museum focuses on contemporary, often abstract art and charges an admission fee to view shows and collections (No admission charge for those under 18). However, its "Critical Dialogue Series," which offers lectures and panel discussions on modern art, is free and open to the public, during which the museum's shows can be viewed for free, too. They are held on Thursday, 6:00 pm to 8:00 pm.

New School for Social Research

Address: 65 Fifth Avenue (between 13th Street and 14th Street)
Phone: (212) 229-5600
Comments: Frequently opens its doors to the public for compelling lectures and panel discussions on contemporary social issues. Past talks included "Organizing the Organized," on the declining influence on labor unions in this country.

New York Academy of Sciences

Address: 2 East 63rd Street
Phone: (212) 838-0230
Comments: The Academy sponsors hundreds of free lectures open to the public on a vast number of scientific topics and issues at its Upper East Side brownstone home. Lectures are usually held in the evenings during the week. Call for upcoming talks.

New York Public Library, Center for the Humanities

Address: Fifth Avenue at 42nd Street
Phone: (212) 340-0833
Comments: Sponsors regular lectures at the main branch as well as its local branches. Call for schedule of events.

New York Society for Ethical Culture

Address: 2 West 64th Street (at Central Park West)
Phone: (212) 874-5210
Comments: Lectures and other events based on civic responsibility and ethical issues, the society is an outgrowth of the late 19th century Ethical Culture Movement. Call for details for events free of charge and open to the public. Past lectures included a panel discussion on crime chaired by Hugh Downs.

New York University

Comments: For NYU's scores of lectures and other events as well, the best place is to look at listings in the school paper, Washington Square News. Also, a useful on-line resource is the NYU events page at: www.nyu.edu/events.

Winston Unity Center

Address: 235 West 23rd Street (between Seventh and Eighth Avenues)
Phone: (212) 924-0550
Comments: A New York hub for Communist Party supporters and enthusiasts, this Center offers a wide range of lectures, exhibitions and panel discussions as well as an archive focused on Marxist doctrine and its influence on the world. Call for free lectures and events.

Libraries

New York City benefits not only from its vibrant public library system, but also from a long list of private libraries, many of which are free and open to the public. The New York Public Library is much more than a repository of books — it is place for workshops, lectures, performances, and is even a crucial tool for small business owners. The private libraries listed in this chapter mostly focus on highly specialized areas.

American Numismatic Society

Address: Broadway (between 155th and 156th Streets)
Open: Tuesday through Saturday, 9:00 am to 4:30 pm; Sunday, 1:00 pm to 4:00 pm
Phone: (212) 234-3130
Comments: Dedicated to the history of money (i.e., minting and bill production), this unique museum's collection houses some one million items and also has an impressive research library. It also accepts coin and archive information inquiries. It is always free and is located in the Audubon Terrace.

Barnard Center for Research on Women

Address: 101 Barnard Hall, 3009 Broadway
Open: Monday through Friday, 9:30 am to 5:00 pm
Phone: (212) 854-2067
Comments: Holds about 20 events per semester including films, readings, lectures and art exhibitions mainly focusing on women's issues, most free and open to the public. Also houses an extensive research library. Call for calendar of events or ask for upcoming activities.

French Institute/Alliance Francaise

Address: 22 East 60th Street
Phone: (212) 355-6100
Comments: This French culture house has a library well-stocked with volumes of French language books, periodicals and newspapers. A good place for francophiles to browse.

Goethe House New York

Address: 1014 Fifth Avenue (at 82nd Street)
Open: Tuesday through Thursday, 9:00 am to 5:00 pm; Saturday, Noon to 5:00 pm (gallery and library hours apply year-round except for summer, when they are closed)
Phone: (212) 439-8700
Comments: This New York arm of the Goethe Institute based in Munich offers the standard found in other branches: changing exhibitions, various cultural events, lectures, films and language instruction (for fee) as well as an extensive library containing some 16,000 German language books, periodicals and recordings.

Kurdish Library and Museum

Address: Park Place at Underhill Avenue, Brooklyn
Open: Monday through Thursday, 1:00 pm to 4:00 pm; Saturday and Sunday, 2:00 pm to 5:00 pm
Phone: (718) 783-7930
Comments: A colorful collection of Kurdish cultural artifacts, traditional dress and arts and crafts giving life to the history of the Kurdish peoples. Also houses a library for researchers.

Library and Museum of the Performing Arts

Address: 111 Amsterdam Avenue (at 65th Street)
Phone: (212) 870-1630
Comments: For an afternoon infusion of solo and ensemble performances, as well as dance, film and theatric works, this Lincoln Center offering is an exceptional opportunity. Tickets are required, but are obtainable an hour before performances. Call for details or drop by for the latest monthly bulletin. The library is very extensive.

New York Historical Society

Address: 170 Central Park West
Phone: (212) 873-3400
Comments: Houses a research library, fine original Audubon watercolors as well as a solid collection of books and other material on the City's history. Lectures and special events, some free of charge.

New York Public Library: Central Research Branch

Address: Fifth Avenue at 42nd Street
Open: Monday through Wednesday, 10:00 am to 9:00 pm; Thursday through Saturday, 10:00 am to 6:00 pm

Phone: (212) 661-7220 (general number)
(212) 869-8089 (for special events)

Comments: New York's hub not only for book lovers, but also for those who need a respite from the harrowing world of mid-town Manhattan. Collections and displays, exhibitions, concerts and lectures transform this library into a museum of sorts. Special collection rooms housing literary treasures include: The Arents Collection in Room 324: early American books; The Berg collection in Room 320: specializing in British & American literature; The Prints Division in Room 308: includes over 180,000 historical prints; rare Book Division in Room 303: houses some of the world's most important books and manuscripts, including a Gutenberg Bible; The Spencer Collection in Room 308: illuminated manuscripts and other important medieval and Gothic period illustrated books. Call main branch, or visit web site for phone numbers and addresses of all local branches, including the newly built, high-tech Science and Business Library (see separate listing below).

New York Public Library of Science and Business

Address: 188 Madison Avenue (between 34th and 35th Streets)
Open: Monday, Friday and Saturday, 10:00 am to 6:00 pm; Tuesday through Thursday, 11:00 am to 7:00 pm
Phone: (212) 592-7000 (choose option four)
Comments: The new, high-tech, Library of Science and Business holds some 200 million volumes, as well as CD ROMs and 100 computer work stations aimed at helping students and professionals with research in the fields of science and business. Free Internet access is available for one hour per day per user. The library also offers free Internet and computer classes.

Literary Events

As the world capital of the publishing industry and with almost as many bookstores as delis, New York is a natural place to experience readings and book signings. There are so many important poets, novelists and other authors reading from their works almost daily, that that they are difficult to keep track of. Many of the selections in this chapter are book stores, which invite local and nationally-known writers to read from their work, and to celebrate newly published books with casual book signings, many of which are free and open to the public. Also, there is ample opportunity to attend poetry readings, which sometime come in the form of "poetry slams" or competitions. Be certain to call for upcoming readings, because many are last-minute. In some cases, calendars of events are offered, so try that, too.

A Different Light

Address: 151 West 19th Street (between Sixth and Seventh Avenues)
Open: 10:00 pm to midnight
Phone: (212) 989-4850
Comments: Regular readings of fiction at this popular Chelsea bookseller. Past readings included activist writer N.A. Diaman reading from Private Nation. Events almost nightly, so call or stop by for a schedule.

Art In The Anchorage

Address: Cadman Plaza, Brooklyn Heights
Open: Spring, Summer and Fall
Phone: (718) 783-1012
Comments: Situated at the base of the Brooklyn Bridge in Brooklyn Heights, this unique site has been converted into an outdoor museum for New York artists, featuring changing exhibitions and sometimes readings, in the "Fiction in the Anchorage" series. Call for details for other readings as well.

Barnes & Noble

Comments: Numerous readings at this chain bookstore's branches throughout the city. Some of the world's most prominent and best selling authors offer free readings and book signings. Look for happenings at the following stores: Chelsea, Upper East Side, Upper West

Side, Union Square and Rockefeller Center, World Trade Center and Lincoln Triangle. Call the Manhattan Barnes & Noble Events Line for daily events and addresses: (212) 727-4810.

Benneton's Cafe

Address: 597 Fifth Avenue (between 48th and 49th Streets)
Phone: (212) 593-0290
Comments: This clothes retailer has begun featuring poetry and fiction readings. Writers featured have included Peter Trachtenber, author of Seven Tatoos. Takes place usually around 6:30 pm about twice a month.

Biblio's

Address: 317 Church Street (between Lispenard and Walker Streets)
Phone: (212) 334-6990
Comments: Throws book readings and signing parties of important poets and writers. Usually holds events two or three times a week at around 7:00 pm on Tuesdays and Thursdays, especially during the academic year, and admission ranges from free to $5. Call for upcoming events.

Blackout Books

Address: 50 Avenue B (between 3rd and 4th Streets)
Phone: (212) 777-1967
Comments: Readings and talks, usually free of charge, at this East Village bookstore known for revolutionary, anarchist literature. Readings are normally at 7:00 pm or 7:30 pm in the evenings.

Borders Books

Address: 1 World Trade Center
Phone: (212) 839-8049
Comments: Borders has fast become one of Manhattan's most important platforms for free lectures and readings by prominent authors. Well-attended. Call or drop by for current and upcoming events at this flagship location and others.

Carpo's Cafe

Address: 189 Bleeker Street at MacDougal Street
Phone: (212) 353-2889
Comments: Free occasional open mike readings at around 8:00 pm. Call for details.

DIA Center for the Arts

Address: 548 West 22nd Street (between Tenth and Eleventh Avenues)
Open: Thursday through Sunday, Noon to 6:00 pm
Phone: (212) 989-5912
Comments: A large, major contemporary art museum, the Center presents changing exhibitions of many established artists, including works by Andy Warhol and Walter de Maria. Exhibits usually are shown for up to a year and are usually quite large installations. Also sponsors "Readings in Contemporary Poetry" series with acclaimed poets and dance performances, some free. Call for details. (Plans to open another space to house its permanent collection at 535 West 22nd Street sometime in 1998).

KGB

Address: 85 East 4th Street (between Second and Third Avenues)
Phone: (212) 505-3360
Comments: Regular readings at this offbeat East Village café/club featuring both well-known and not-so-well-known poets. Held Mondays at around 8:30 pm, but call to confirm.

Lenox Hill Bookstore

Address: 1018 Lexington Avenue (at 73rd Street)
Phone: (212) 472-7170
Comments: A popular Upper East Side bookseller which hosts free readings and signings about four or five times a month, usually around 6:30 pm. Past readings included Laurence Bergreen, author of "Louis Armstrong: An Extravagant Life."

National Arts Club

Address: 15 Gramercy Park South (between Park Avenue South and Irving Place)
Phone: (212) 475-3424
Comments: Sponsors regular fiction and poetry readings free and open to the public. Past series have included poets Timothy Houghton and Elizabeth Sydel Morgan. Though private, this wonderful old establishment with a noble history of promoting the arts also generously hosts art exhibitions free to the public.

New York Public Library

Address: Fifth Avenue at 42nd Street
Open: Monday through Wednesday, 10:00 am to 9:00 pm; Thursday through Saturday, 10.00 am to 6:00 pm.
Phone: (212) 661-7220 (general number)
(212) 869-8089 (for special events)
Comments: The New York Public Library often sponsors poetry reading, workshops and discussion groups relating to literature at its branches throughout the city. Call for details, or drop by the central branch for listings of events.

New York University

Address: 566 LaGuardia Place
Phone: (212) 998-5424
Comments: Call or visit the Loeb Student Center to find listings and postings of free readings of poetry and fiction.

Nuyorican Poets Cafe

Address: 236 East Third Street (between Avenues B and C)
Phone: (212) 505-8183
Comments: Poetry readings frequently are central to the entertainment of this aptly named East Village café.

NYC Poetry Calendar

Address: 60 East 4th Street
New York, NY 10003
Phone: (212) 260-7097
Comments: An extensive list of poetry readings and events all over the city, many free. It is distributed in many bookstores, or obtained at some of the public libraries. Or, order it for a modest fee at the above address.

Peacock, The

Address: 24 Greenwich Street (between Sixth and Seventh Avenues)
Phone: (212) 242-9395
Comments: Holds free poetry readings every Tuesday around 7:00 pm at this old-world Italian café.

Poetry Society of America

Address: 15 Gramercy Park
Phone: (212) 254-9628
Comments: America's oldest poetry organization, the Poetry Society of America is responsible for the "Poetry in Motion" program, which displays poems in subways and buses as well as "Poetry in Public Places," which presents readings all over the city. Call for details on free readings.

Poets House

Address: 72 Spring Street (between Crosby and Lafayette Streets)
Phone: (212) 431-7920
Comments: Holds readings, lectures and book exhibitions occasionally open free to the public.

Shakespeare & Co.

Address: 939 Lexington Avenue (between 68th and 69th Streets)
Open: 9:00 am to 8:30 pm
Phone: (212) 570-0201
Comments: One of the city's most important booksellers; holds mostly fiction readings by highly regarded authors and occasionally work by poets at its two stores.

Teachers and Writers Collaborative

Address: 5 Union Square West (between 14th and 15th Streets)
Phone: (212) 691-6590
Comments: Devoted to nurturing the careers of emerging and established writers and teachers, the collaborative has among its founding members, Phillip Levine and Denise Levertov. Call for free events and readings.

Village Comics

Address: 214 Sullivan Street (between Bleeker and West Third Streets)
Phone: (212) 777-2770
Comments: Signings and appearances by comic book writers as well as authors of science fiction.

Writer's Voice, The

Address: 5 West 63rd Street
Phone: (212) 875-4124
Comments: Sponsors readings of poetry and fiction, some for free.

Meditation

While most places for organized meditation practices charge a usually modest fee, some welcome visitors free of charge. This may not be an exhaustive list, but it includes a solid base for such places. Most offer specialized classes for a fee, and all have trained personnel to help you shut out the city and find greater well-being.

Himalayan Institute of New York – Columbus Avenue

Address: 568 Columbus Avenue (at 88th Street)
Open: Monday through Saturday, 10:00 am to 7:00 pm; Sunday, 11:00 am to 7:00 pm
Phone: (212) 787-7552
Comments: Hosts a number of workshops and classes on holistic health practices and techniques, including free meditation classes on Thursdays from 6:00 pm to 7:00 pm at both its Columbus Avenue and Fifth Avenue locations.

Himalayan Institute of New York – Fifth Avenue

Address: 78 Fifth Avenue (at 14th Street)
Open: Monday through Friday, 1:00 pm to 5:00 pm
Phone: (212) 243-5995
Comments: See above listing.

New York Open Center

Address: 83 Spring Street
Open: Monday through Saturday, 9:30 am to 10:00 pm; Sunday, 9:00 am to 6:00 pm
Phone: (212) 219-2527
Comments: Meditation room is free of charge. Also, sponsors "open houses" three times a year, which include day-long "sample classes" from the Center's hundreds of classes on holistic learning and culture. Those who volunteer at the Center can take classes for free. In addition, the Center offers free magazines on holistic issues.

New York Shambhala Center

Address: 118 West 22nd Street, 6th floor
Phone: (212) 675-6544
Comments: Dedicated to Tibetan Buddhism and the teachings of Shambhala, this center offers classes and programs for a fee, but also opens its meditation room free of charge and offers a free meditation instruction class every Tuesday at 6:30 pm and Sunday at 11:00 am. In addition, it offers meditation consultation free of charge, as well as free "public" mediation sessions from 6:00 pm to 7:30 pm Monday through Friday and Sunday afternoons.

Museums

One could spend weeks visiting New York's museums without spending a dime on admission. What makes many of these museums so alluring is their quirkiness: places like the Police Academy Museum, Lower East Side Tenement Museum, the Museum of Financial History or the Con Edison Energy Museum. Others are more traditional, like the Guggenheim, the Museum of Modern Art, and the National Museum of the American Indian, which have special free days.

Noticeably absent are places like the New York Metropolitan Museum, which ask for suggested donations. While you probably won't be thrown out for not paying something for a ticket, you might get an understandably chilly response. Others have "Pay What You Wish" admission policies which are included in our selection. Also, keep an eye out for Museum Mile Festival, usually held in June when, for a day, most museums along Fifth Avenue and elsewhere throw their doors open free of admission charge.

Alice Austen House

Address: 2 Hylen Boulevard Avenue at Bay Street, Staten Island
Open: Thursday through Sunday, Noon to 5:00 pm
Phone: (718) 816-4506
Comments: Preserved home of Alice Austen, a famous turn-of-the-century Staten Island photographer, this museum offers free events to the public, but the main attraction is the collection of Austen's experimental and documentary photographs taken in the U.S. and abroad. Closed January and February.

American Numismatic Society

Address: Broadway between 155th and 156th Streets
Open: Tuesday through Saturday, 9:00 am to 4:30 pm; Sunday, 1:00 pm to 4:00 pm
Phone: (212) 234-3130
Comments: Dedicated to the history of money (i.e, minting and bill production), this unique museum holds some one million items and also has an impressive research library. It also accepts coin and archive information inquiries.

Art Directors Club

Address: 250 Park Avenue South (at 20th Street)
Phone: (212) 674-0500
Comments: Organizes changing exhibitions with intriguing themes, like "Contemporary Slovenian Graphic Design," which showcased leading designers from Slovenia, and "Young Guns NYC," a collection of work by young graphic designers and photographers.

Bronx Museum of the Arts

Address: 1040 Grand Concourse (at 165th Street)
Open: Wednesday, 3:00 pm to 9:00 pm; Thursday and Friday, 10:00 am to 5:00 pm; Saturday and Sunday, 1:00 pm to 6:00 pm
Phone: (718) 681-6000
Comments: An important cultural center in the Bronx, and home to changing exhibitions, some from local artists.

Brooklyn Children's Museum

Address: 145 Brooklyn Avenue, Brooklyn
Open: Summer Hours: Monday, Wednesday, Thursday, Saturday and Sunday, Noon to 5:00 pm; Friday, Noon to 6:30 pm
Winter Hours: Wednesday through Friday, 2:00 pm to 5:00 pm; Saturday and Sunday, Noon to 5:00 pm
Phone: (718) 735-4400
Comments: Founded in 1899, this museum is billed as the world's first museum designed just for children. Exhibitions emphasize learning and building self-confidence through hands-on displays. The museum includes workshops and a library. Its newest home, a 35,000 square foot facility, sponsors innovative programs aimed at teaching children history as well about social and technological changes in contemporary life. Every day there is a suggested donation, but it is not obligatory. During summer, rooftop performances are offered on Friday evenings.

Brooklyn's History Museum

Address: 128 Pierrepont Street, Brooklyn Heights, Brooklyn
Open: Monday, Thursday, Friday and Saturday, Noon to 5:00 pm
Phone: (718) 624-0890
Comments: The coveted depository of Brooklyn's past, this museum houses countless pieces of Brooklyn artifacts, photographs and architectural peices reflecting one of the country's most colorful cities. The museum includes four permanent exhibition spaces, dedicated to Brooklyn themes, like the Dodgers and the Brooklyn Bridge. Free on Mondays only. It plans to close for renovations in mid-1998 through the

beginning of 1999. Call to confirm that plan.

Con Edison Energy Museum

Address: 145 East 14th Street (at Third Avenue)
Open: Tuesday through Saturday, 9:00 am to 5:00 pm
Phone: (212) 460-6244
Comments: An in-depth look at the history and science of electricity, highlighting discoveries and inventions of Thomas Edison. Offers a re-created tour through an underground New York City street to demonstrate the intricate matrix of wiring, as well as a passing subway car. Film, photographs, models and original antique contraptions also help illuminate the history of electricity.

Cooper Hewitt Museum

Address: 2 East 91st Street
Open: Monday, Wednesday through Friday, 10:00 am to 5:00 pm; Sunday, Noon to 5:00 pm; Tuesday, 10:00 am to 9:00 pm. Free on Tuesdays, 5:00 pm to 9:00 pm
Phone: (212) 849-8400
Comments: Housed in a turn-of-the-century Carnegie mansion, this museum is dedicated to architecture, and is run under the auspices of The Smithsonian Institution. It is free of charge on Tuesday, 5:00 pm to 9:00 pm.

Dyckman Farmhouse Museum

Address: 4881 Broadway (at West 204th Street)
Open: Tuesday through Sunday, 11:00 am to 4:00 pm. Call first.
Phone: (212) 304-9422
Comments: Billed as Manhattan's oldest colonial farmhouse, the Dyckman farmhouse currently standing was built in 1784, and was preceded by one built in 1662. It includes Revolutionary War relics and a replica of a revolutionary war military hut in a garden behind the house, built from materials found in an archeological dig in Manhattan.

Ellis Island Immigration Museum

Address: Ellis Island, New York Harbor
Open: Open daily year-round from 9:30 am to 5:00 pm with extended hours in the summer. Closed Christmas Day.

Statue of Liberty and Ellis Island ferries leave from Battery Park and from Liberty State Park, New Jersey, running about every 30 to 45

minutes beginning at 9:15 am (call (212) 269-5755 for details.
Phone: (212) 363-7620

Comments: Having welcomed newly arrived immigrants for over six decades until closed for processing immigration in 1954, Ellis Island is currently a major tourist draw. It houses a museum in The Great Hall, where immigrants waited for their entry to be processed and approved. Offers free films and over 25 exhibits on the history of the American immigrant through artifacts, music, photographs, etc. Also on the island are: Ellis Island galleries with changing exhibitions, the Ellis Island Immigration Museum, and a memorial Wall. Entrance to the island is free, but there is a charge for the ferry from Manhattan.

Fashion Institute of Technology Museum

Address: Seventh Avenue at West 27th Street
Open: Tuesday through Friday, Noon to 8:00 pm; Saturday, 10:00 am to 5:00 pm
Phone: (212) 217-5848

Comments: An outstanding collection of clothes and textiles dating from the 19th century to the present, FIT holds exhibitions from its massive collection of clothes as well as photographs and documents chronicaling the history of design.

Federal Hall National Memorial

Address: 26 Wall Street (at Nassau Street)
Open: Monday through Friday, 9:00 am to 5:00 pm.
Phone: (212) 825-6888

Comments: One of America's most important historical buildings, the original Federal Hall built on this site was one of the first seats of Congress. It was also the site where George Washington took his first oath as president. The building that stands today was built in 1842, and was used as an U.S. Customs building. It has a stunning rotunda, period furniture and documentation reflecting the rich history of the site, New York and the country's history.

Garibaldi-Meucci Museum, The

Address: 420 Thompkins Avenue, Staten Island
Open: Tuesday through Friday, 1:00 pm to 5:00 pm
Phone: (718) 442-1608

Comments: A farmhouse with personal belongings of Antonio Meucci, an Italian emigrant credited as the actual inventor of the telephone. Meucci lived a modest life as a candle maker and invited his friend Giuseppe Garibaldi, a hero of the Italian Liberation, to live with him in

New York for a number of years in the 1850s.

George Gustav Heye Center of the Smithsonian's National Museum of the American Indian
Address: 1 Bowling Green
Open: 10:00 am to 5:00 pm, open every day, Thursday, until 8:00 pm
Phone: (212) 668-6624
Comments: Dedicated to preserving and exhibiting artifacts of American Indian culture, its history and traditions through displays as well as performances. Houses more than one million items from the U.S. as well as from Latin America and Canada. This free-of-charge institution in the Wall Street district also hosts dancers, artists and elders and story tellers.

Interchurch Center
Address: 475 Riverside Drive (at West 120th Street)
Open: Monday through Friday, 9:00 am to 4:30 pm.
Phone: (212) 870-2200
Comments: Focusing on the harmonious cooperation and co-existence of Christian faiths, the Center holds changing exhibitions on Christian themes.

Isamo Noguchi Garden Museum
Address: 32-37 Vernon Boulevard (at 10th Street), Long Island City, Queens.
Open: Wednesday and Saturday, Noon to 5:00 pm
Phone: (718) 204-7088
Comments: With a mission to preserve and show over six decades of the work of Noguchi, this museum includes sculptures in metal and stone among its over 250 pieces. The works are housed in 12 galleries and a beautiful and tranquil sculpture garden. Open from April 1st to end of October.

Jewish Museum, The
Address: 1109 Fifth Avenue (at 92nd Street)
Open: Sunday, Monday, Wednesday and Thursday, 11:00 am to 5:45 pm; Tuesday, 11:00 am to 8:00 pm. Free Tuesdays 5:00 pm to 8:00 pm
Phone: (212) 423-3200
Comments: Chronicles the history and cultures of the Jewish peoples, with an exhaustive permanent collection of photographs, documents and film, with much devoted to the Holocaust, its victims and its survi-

vors. Also, hosts changing exhibitions, most of them closely related to Jewish history and traditions. Free admission on Tuesdays, 5:00 pm to 8:00 pm.

Kurdish Library and Museum

Address: 144 Underhill Avenue at Park place, Brooklyn
Open: Monday through Thursday, 1:00 pm to 4:00 pm; Saturday and Sunday, 2:00 pm to 5:00 pm
Phone: (718) 783-7930
Comments: A colorful collection of Kurdish cultural artifacts, traditional dress and arts and crafts giving life to the history of the Kurdish peoples. Also houses a library for researchers.

Lower East Side Tenement Museum

Address: 97 Orchard Street
Open: Tuesday through Friday, 11:00 am to 4:00 pm; Sunday, 10:00 am to 4:00 pm
Phone: (212) 431-0233
Comments: Preserving the spirit of New York's tenements, where many of the city's immigrants lived through the decades, this museum pays tribute to the rich traditions and cultures brought to New York by various ethnic groups through documents, film, theater, art and memorabilia. While the bulk of the museum's offerings come in the form of tours (for fee) through creative reenactments of early 20th century tenement life, it does allow visitors to view its gallery free of charge, but call in advance to make an appointment. Also, it holds occasional free special events like films and performances reflecting tenement life.

Municipal Art Society's Urban Center

Address: 457 Madison Avenue (between 50th and 51st Street)
Open: Monday, Tuesday, Wednesday and Friday, 11:00 am to 5:00 pm
Phone: (212) 935-3960
Comments: Formed by the Municipal Art Society, a group established in 1893 to improve New York's state of public art, the center is devoted to preserving and expanding the city's buildings and parks. Holds lectures and public events to this end. Also, offers a gallery with changing exhibitions related to its mission.

Museum of African American History and Art

Address: Adam Clayton Powell, Jr., State Office Building, 163 West 125th Street, 2nd floor
Phone: (212) 749-5298

Comments: Home to a large collection of film works (some 6,000), the Museum of African American History and Art also features changing exhibitions in its gallery as well as a free annual conference centering on its film archives. Holds about 200 cultural and arts events ranging from free to $4. Call ahead for hours, which vary and usually accommodate only special events.

Museum of American Financial History

Address: 28 Broadway
Open: Monday through Friday, 11:30 am to 3:30 pm
Phone: (212) 908-4110
Comments: Focused on preserving rare items related to this country's capital markets and to the history of our financial systems, this smallish one-floor museum is a popular stop for tourists and New Yorkers interested in the underpinnings of Wall Street and financial institutions.

Museum of Modern Art

Address: 11 West 53rd Street (between Fifth and Sixth Avenues)
Open: Free (Pay What You Wish) Friday, 4:30 pm to 8:30 pm. Other hours: Saturday through Tuesday, Thursday, 10:30 am to 6:00 pm
Phone: (212) 708-9480
Comments: One of the world's most important museums, MOMA possesses a collection of over 100,000 pieces, with a strong emphasis on abstract paintings and sculptures. Also shows films from its large archive of modern cinematic works. On Fridays, from 4:30 pm to 8:30 pm, MOMA holds its "Pay What You Wish" nights, which could be interpreted as meaning free (if that is what you wish).

National Academy of Design

Address: 1083 Fifth Avenue (between 89th and 90th Streets)
Open: Wednesday through Sunday, Noon to 5:00 pm; Friday, noon to 8:00 pm (Free 5:00 pm to 8:00 pm, Fridays)
Phone: (212) 369-4880
Comments: An alluring mix of contemporary and traditional art and design, the museum also holds eclectic changing exhibitions. Free on Fridays, 5:00 pm to 8:00 pm

New York Hall of Science

Address: 47-01 111th Street, Flushing Meadows-Corona Park, Queens
Open: Tuesday and Wednesday, 9:30 am to 2:00 pm; Thursday and Friday, 9:00 am to 5:00 pm; Saturday and Sunday, 11:00 am to 5:00 pm

Phone: (718) 699 0675

Comments: Dedicated to enlivening physics and biology education through compelling interactive and hands-on exhibitions. Also features outdoor science playground (flat shoes required), and special exhibitions, like a glowing model of a brain, 12 times normal size. Free on Fridays, from 2:00 pm to 5:00 pm.

New York Unearthed

Address: 17 State Street (between Whitehall and Pearl Streets)
Open: Monday through Saturday, Noon to 6:00 pm
Phone: (212) 748-8600
Comments: This museum, while geared to children, may also be of interest to parents as well. It focuses on past and current archeological digs carried out in New York City, and even has its own on-going sample dig sight behind glass to allow visitors to see diggers work. Also has an elevator providing a glimpse of a simulated descent from a city street down to the city's bowels.

Newseum/NY

Address: 580 Madison Avenue (at 56th Street)
Open: Monday through Saturday, 10:00 am to 5:30 pm
Phone: (212) 317-6500
Comments: Funded by The Freedom Forum, the international free press watchdog group, Newseum/NY is a branch of the Washington D.C.-based Newseum. Exhibits, lectures, films, focusing on all media, and issues pertaining to free press and expression. It features an "Author Series", which focus on news-related books, and has included Walter Cronkite.

Nicholas Roerich Museum

Address: 319 West 107th Street
Open: Tuesday through Sunday, 2:00 pm to 5:00 pm
Phone: (212) 864-7752
Comments: Home to thousands of works of art collected by artist-philosopher Nicholas Roerich, including frescoes and paintings. Also hosts lectures, chamber music performances and poetry readings, as well as changing art exhibitions. Contributions are voluntary.

Police Academy Museum

Address: 235 East 20th Street
Open: Monday through Friday, 9:00 am to 3:00 pm

Phone: (212) 477-9753
Comments: A salvo of fine artifacts and memorabilia (uniforms, guns, pistols, clubs) along with historical documents chronicling the New York Police Department's long history. Also includes artifacts from other U.S. and foreign police departments.

Queens County Farm Museum

Address: 73-50 Little Neck Parkway in Floral Park, Queens.
Open: 9:00 am to 5:00 pm daily (farmhouse and museum galleries, 10:00 am to 5:00 pm on weekends)
Phone: (718) 347-3276
Comments: New York City's only continuously working farm, Queens County farm boasts cows, goats, peacocks and a chicken coop on its 47 acres. Also sells farm-fresh eggs for $2 a dozen. Holds free hay rides as well as other children's events, like colonial cooking. Some special events are not free, so call ahead.

Salmagundi Club

Address: 47 Fifth Avenue
Open: 1:00 pm to 5:00 pm daily, including Saturday and Sunday
Phone: (212) 255-7740
Comments: A non-profit organization dedicated to supporting painting, photography, sculpture and art appreciation. Founded over a century ago, the Club is housed in a grand landmark building near Washington Square Park. It welcomes members — and asks for dues — but opens its doors daily to its free exhibitions.

School of Visual Arts Museum

Address: School of Visual Arts, 209 East 23rd Street (between Second and Third Avenues)
Open: Monday, Wednesday and Friday, 9:00 am to 6:30 pm; Thursday, 9:00 am to 8:00 pm; Saturday, 10:00 am to 5:00 pm
Phone: (212) 592-2144
Comments: Holds changing exhibitions, many drawn from the work of students. Past exhibitions included "11111001101," a collection of work from the school's computer art students. Shows also include veteran artists, like those featured in the school's annual "Masters Series."

Seventh Regiment Armory

Address: Park Avenue (between 66th and 67th Streets)
Phone: (212) 744-8180

Comments: Houses some Civil War artifacts and other articles pertaining to military history. Call to reserve a time for a tour.

Skyscraper Museum

Address: 44 Wall Street (near Williams Street) — temporary home
Open: Tuesday through Saturday, Noon to 6:00 pm
Phone: (212) 968-1961
Comments: This financial district museum is a repository of photographs, architectural drafts, building models and maps chronicling the spectacular history of the skyscraper. It is free of admission charge, but there is a donation bowl in which visitors may contribute. Call for information also on free lectures and gallery and walking tours. The museum will likely change location in 1998, so call to confirm.

Solomon R. Guggenheim Museum

Address: 1071 Fifth Avenue (at 89th Street)
Open: Sunday through Wednesday, 10:00 am to 6:00 pm; Friday and Saturday, 10:00 am to 8:00 pm. Pay what you wish on Fridays, 6:00 pm to 8:00 pm
Phone: (212) 423-3500
Comments: One of the most popular destinations on museum mile, this Frank Lloyd Wright designed landmark is home to some of the world's most enduring and important works of modern art. It also opens its doors on Friday evenings to those less inclined to pay full admission. Billed as "Pay What You Wish Night" on Fridays, 6:00 pm to 8:00 pm visitors are technically allowed to enter free of charge. Collection includes some of the most important works by Miro, Picasso and Kandinsky.

South Street Seaport Museum

Address: 207 Front Street (at Fulton Street)
Open: Monday through Sunday 10:00 am to 5:00 pm. Until 6:00 pm during the summer.
Phone: (212) 748-8600
Comments: Located in the recently developed Wall Street area waterfront, the museum illuminates the mercantile and shipping history of this famous port. Also hosts films, lectures, festivals, and special events. Call for details on free special events. Also, the area includes scores of retail stores and eateries, as well as free outdoor concerts.

Statue of Liberty National Monument and Museum

Address: Liberty Island, New York Harbor

Open. Monument opened daily year round from 9:30 am to 5:00 pm with extended hours in the summer. Closed Christmas Day.

Statue of Liberty and Ellis Island ferries leave from Battery Park and from Liberty State Park, New Jersey, running about every 30 to 45 minutes beginning at 9:15 am (call (212) 269-5755 for details).

Phone: (212) 363-7620

Comments: Perhaps the city's most popular tourist destination, the Statue of Liberty was built in 1886 and designed by Frederic Bartholdi. The 151-foot gift from France attracts over 4 million visitors a year. Inside, some 350 steps lead to the crown of the statue, which affords one of the city's most spectacular views.

Whitney Museum at Philip Morris

Address: 120 Park Avenue

Open: Monday through Friday, 11:00 am to 6:00 pm; Thursday, closes at 7:30 pm

Phone: (212) 878-2453

Comments: Based in the Philip Morris headquarters, this museum offers changing exhibitions of modern art and sculptures by American artists. Another arm of the Whitney Museum of American Art.

Whitney Museum of American Art

Address: 945 Madison Avenue (at 75th Street)

Open: Wednesday, Friday, Saturday and Sunday, 11:00 am to 6:00 pm; Thursday, 1:00 pm to 8:00 pm

Phone: (212) 570- 3600

Comments: One of the city's altars of contemporary American art, the Whitney holds cutting edge and often controversial shows in addition to its impressive permanent collection which represents just about every major American artist. Free on Thursdays 6:00 pm to 8:00 pm.

NYC Web Sites

As web sites proliferate, it is difficult to keep track of new ones coming on-line. This short list should provide a good base from which to ferret out anything you need to know about New York events. As they pertain to free events and services, these sites may also serve as a helpful way to find updated information described in this book.

Arts Wire

Address: www.artswire.com
Comments: Provides information on artist organizations, galleries and individual artists in New York City and nationally. Provides an in-depth calendar of events.

DowntownNY.com

Address: www.DowntownNY.com
Comments: Focused on round-the-clock business, residential and tourist information on the Downtown area.

Marco Polo City Listings

Address: www.marcopolo.com/cities
Comments: Nuts-and-bolts site includes information on city news and other useful items, particularly related to fashion.

New York sidewalk.com

Address: www.newyork.sidewalk.com
Comments: A fresh look for information on virtually all aspects of New York, plus good leads on other sources on the Internet.

New York City Citysearch

Address: www.citysearch.com
Comments: One of the most comprehensive sites for entertainment and restaurants. Very easy to use, and frequently updated.

New York Web

Address: www.nywb.com
Comments: Extensive listings of events and happenings in the city,

with emphasis on pop culture and the club scene.

The NYCInsider

Address: www.theinsider.com
Comments: Great site for information on shopping, tours, sightseeing and links to other related sites.

Village Voice

Address: www.villagevoice.com
Comments: Mirrors the newspaper's exhaustive listings of events and nightlife goings-on.

Outdoor Performances

As New York becomes safer and more pedestrian friendly, the number of outdoor performances, especially in the warmer months, has risen appreciably. Most are in the form of festivals, and take place on weekends. Some, like SummerStage, have already become institutions. Most take place in parks, where throngs of visitors come with a beach blanket and lunch basket in tow. Almost every type of music and dance is represented, as the list below illustrates.

BACA's Summer Celebration

Address: The following parks have been included in the series: Bensonhurst Park, Cuyler Gore Park, John Paul Jones Park, Commodore J. Barry Park, Pierrepont Street Playground, Linden Park, Marine Park, Kaiser Park, Carroll Park, and Red Hook Community Center. Call for details.

Phone: BACA/The Brooklyn Arts Council, 195 Cadman Plaza West, Brooklyn, (718) 625-0080

Comments: Sponsored by BACA/The Brooklyn Arts Council, Summer Celebration organizes free outdoor concerts, dance performances, clowning, storytelling and other events in Brooklyn Parks in June and July.

BAM/City Parks Outside

Address: Fort Greene Park, Linden Park, Von King/Tompkins Park and Sternberg/Lindsey Park

Phone: (212) 360-8288

Comments: Organizes free outdoor concerts at four Brooklyn parks, featuring rock, popular and classical bands in July and August on Tuesdays, Wednesdays and Thursdays, depending on the park. Call for details.

BAMoutside Music at MetroTech

Address: MetroTech, in the Civic Center/Borough Hall area of downtown Brooklyn

Phone: (718) 636-4100

Comments: For five years, the Brooklyn Academy of Music has presented outdoor shows throughout the summer at MetroTech, situated in the Civic Center/Borough Hall area of downtown Brooklyn. Performances have included: Rhythm & Blues Stars of New Orleans, The Marvellettes & The Chiffons and Lesley Gore. Shows in the past have been at noon and 1:00 pm. Call for details.

Bryant Park

Address: 42nd Street between Fifth and Sixth Avenues
Phone: (212) 983-4143
Comments: This recently restored park, now one of Manhattan's most stately spots, is home to a vast number of events. Included are: Monday night films at dusk during the summer, a Young Artist Concert Series, as well as many other concerts sprinkled throughout the season. Most notable are: the free lunch and after-work performances and the New Work New York, Jazz at Dusk and The Johnny Mercer Foundation Celebrates Broadway series, clustered between May and September. Call Events Hot Line at (212) 922-9393.

Buskers Fare

Address: City Hall, World Trade Center, Trinity Church, Chase Plaza, Broad Street, South Street Seaport, Pace Downtown Theater
Phone: (212) 432-0900
Comments: The Buskers Fare, going on for five years, is an international festival of street artists held at various Lower Manhattan locations (e.g., South Street Seaport, World Trade Center, Trinity Church, Chase Plaza) in early June. See performers of all stripes: puppeteers, dancers, percussionists, and jugglers. In the past: The Artful Juggler, The New Way Circus, Five Chinese Brothers and X-Cheerleaders. Sponsored by the Lower Manhattan Cultural Council. Call ahead for information.

Castle Clinton Concerts, Battery Park

Address: Battery Park
Phone: (212) 344-7220
Comments: Hosts summer evening concerts at historic Castle Clinton Park at Manhattan's southern-most tip, with views of the Statue of Liberty and Ellis Island and Wall Street's wall of buildings. Performances have included John Mayall and the Frank Sinatra, Jr. Orchestra. Held July and August usually at 6:00 pm.

Celebrate Brooklyn

Address: Borough Hall Plaza, Brooklyn Heights, Brooklyn
Phone: (718) 625-0080
Comments: Features performances which have included Spalding Gray and offbeat musical bands in the summer months. Call for details.

Central Park

Phone: (212) 360-3456; Also, for other events and general information on Central Park, call (212) 794-6564
Comments: Central Park Special Events Hotline is a useful source to hear the latest goings-on in Central Park, including SummerStage (see Outdoor Performances chapter) concerts, festivals, etc.

Lehman College

Address: Bedford Park Boulevard, The Bronx
Open: Monday, Tuesday, Thursday, Friday, from 10:00 am to 5:00 pm
Phone: (718) 960-8000
Comments: Holds numerous outdoor free concerts, as well as other performing arts, in the summer.

Museum of Modern Art's Summergarden

Address: MOMA Sculpture Garden, 54th Street
Phone: (212) 708-9491
Comments: Held in MOMA's Sculpture Garden, this series of concerts is open to the public under the "Pay What You Wish" policy and takes place Fridays and Saturdays from June to August at 8:30 pm.

New York Philharmonic

Phone: (212) 875-5700 for 1998 summer information
Comments: One of the world's most important orchestras plays free of charge in parks through the five boroughs throughout the summer. Call for details.

Out-of-Doors Festival

Address: Amsterdam Avenue (at 62nd Street)
Phone: (212) 875-5108
Comments: For 27 seasons, Lincoln Center has thrown this free festival for the public free of charge at Damrosch Park's Guggenheim Bandshell, and in and around Lincoln Center. Featuring big bands, dance ensembles and other musical groups. Past events included Brazilfest '97, Irish band Sine and chamber music. Call for schedule of events,

usually available in June for that summer.

Prospect Park
Address: Prospect Park, Brooklyn, near Grand Army Plaza and the Public Library
Open: Monday through Friday, 9:00 am to 5:00 pm
Phone: (718) 965-8900
Comments: Brooklyn's answer to Central Park, Prospect Park holds many free outdoor classical and jazz concerts and performances in the summer. Call for details, or ask for calendar mailing.

Seuffert Bandshell
Address: Forest Park Music Grove, Forest Park, Woodhaven, Queens
Phone: (718) 235-4100
Comments: Home to many summer events including the Queens Symphony Orchestra, and a mixed bag of ethnic bands, the Seuffert Bandshell is a big draw in Queens, where it is set in idyllic Forest Park in Woodhaven.

Sounds at Sunset at the Battery Park Esplanade
Address: Battery Park, Lower Manhattan
Phone: (212) 416-5300 or (212) 267-9700
Comments: Evening concerts from June through August, featuring a string of different musical performances at Battery Park, with arresting views of the harbor and the Statue of Liberty. Call for details.

Sounds on the Hudson
Phone: (212) 416-5328
Comments: Free concerts by Hispanic musicians in September in celebration of Hispanic Heritage month. Past artists featured included: Johnny Pacheo, Jose Fajardo and Pupi Lagarrete. Call for details.

South Street Seaport/Pier 17
Address: South Street and Fulton Streets
Phone: (212) 732-7678
Comments: Spring, summer and fall free concerts featuring a wide array of music, usually in the evenings in the historic seaport/Wall Street area with romantic views of the Brooklyn Bridge and Brooklyn Heights across the harbor. Call events hotline for details.

SummerMusic, Bronx Arts Ensemble

Address: c/o Golf House, Van Cortlandt Park, Bronx
Phone: (718) 601-7399
Comments: For 25 years, the Bronx Arts Ensemble has sponsored this series of free concerts in July and August which have included an eclectic assortment: from brass quintets to baroque chamber music to Latino bands. Concerts are performed twice at two different locations: The Bronx's Van Cortland Park and McGinley Center of Fordham University.

SummerStage

Address: Rumsey Playfield, Central Park, near 72nd Street entrance
Open: Throughout the summer (June through August), Wednesday through Friday, 8:30 pm; Weekend, 3:00 pm
Phone: (212) 360-2777 or the hotline at (212) 360-CPSS
Comments: Myriad events including rock concerts, readings, symphonies, operas and dance, draw thousands to Central Park's Rumsey Playfield, situated close to the 72nd Street entrance. Past acts have included: Garth Brooks, New York Grand Opera, Bruce Cockburn, Tom Chapin, and Buckwheat Zydeco.

Union Square Summer Series

Address: Union Square Park, Broadway at 17th Street
Open: Noon
Phone: (212) 360-8111 or (212) 360-3456
Comments: A smattering of different band sounds — from jazz to reggae — fills Union Square during the summer months, usually beginning at noon. Call for specifics.

Washington Square Music Festival

Address: Washington Square Park
Phone: (212) 431-1088
Comments: Weekly concerts held at Washington Square Park's Garibaldi Statue, on Tuesday nights at 8:00 pm during June, July and August. Call for details, for dates may vary.

Parks

The City's parks have become much more than a place to stroll. They are centers for educational workshops, a brew of sports activities from roller-blading to cricket, as well as stages for all sorts of artistic and cultural events. Listed here are among the finest of the city's public parks and park organizations.

Belvedere Castle

Address: Central Park, near 79th Street and south of the Great Lawn.
Open: Visitor's Center open Tuesday through Sunday, 11:00 am to 4:00 pm
Phone: (212) 772-0210
Comments: A hub of Central Park, and a great place to bring children, the medieval-design castle is an educational center for adults and children, sponsoring nature exhibits on geology, park history and wildlife as well as many types of entertainment. It is the base for the city's Urban Park Rangers and is also New York's National Weather Service Station.

Bryant Park

Address: 40th to 42nd Streets (between Fifth Avenue and Avenue of the Americas)
Phone: (212) 983-4142
Comments: One of Manhattan's jewels, Bryant Park is located behind the main Fifth Avenue branch of the New York Public Library. The park possesses meticulously-maintained flower beds as well as a sizable lawn for sun bathing or picnicking. Also home to free movies and concerts.

Castle Clinton Park

Address: Battery Park
Phone: (212) 344-7220
Comments: Situated at Manhattan's southern-most tip, with views of the Statue of Liberty and Ellis Island and Wall Street's wall of buildings. The red stone defense structure was built before the War of 1812, and attracts picnickers and tourists. Also holds concerts at mid-day during the summer.

Central Park/ Central Park Conservancy

Address: The Arsenal, Central Park, 830 Fifth Avenue
Phone: (212) 360-8111
Comments: A private, non-profit organization formed in 1980 to help manage Central Park with the City of New York. Helps host numerous free programs throughout the year at: The Charles A. Dana Discovery Center, Belvedere Castle (The Henry Luce Nature Observatory) and The Dairy (see individual listings for these). Highlights include a spate of free art and nature discovery programs throughout the year, as well as weekend and family workshops. Request the quarterly calendar of events for a list of happenings in Central Park.

Prospect Park

Address: Main entrance situated near Grand Army Plaza and Public Library in Park Slope, Brooklyn.
Open: Open dawn to dusk
Phone: (718) 965-8999 (general information); (718) 788-0055 (Wollman Rink)
Comments: On the edge of Brooklyn's Park Slope neighborhood, Prospect Park can be thought of as Central Park's Brooklyn cousin. Designed by Frederick Law Olmstead and Calvert Vaux in the late 1860s, the park attracts soccer pick-up games, picnic outings, and even horseback riders. The park, on over 500 acres of fields, hills, ponds and forest, also offers ice skating at the Wollman Rink (for a fee), and is home to numerous concerts and other cultural events.

Staten Island Botanical Garden

Address: 1000 Richmond Terrace, Staten Island
Open: Monday through Friday, 9:00 am to 5:00 pm
Phone: (718) 273-8200
Comments: Wonderful arrangement of gardens, rare plants, ponds and unusual trees as well as a greenhouse.

Van Cortlandt Park

Address: North-Central Bronx, bordering Westchester County
Comments: The Bronx's oasis, this park covers nearly two square miles and features facilities for boating, picnicking, tennis, softball and cricket. The nearby Van Corlandt Golf Course (for fee) adds to the park's attraction. Call for free cultural events.

Pets

Free pets from animal shelters are almost non-existent in metropolitan New York shelters. This is mainly so because shelters need the assurance that prospective owners are serious enough to commit at least a nominal initial investment. North Shore Animal League, on Long Island breaks this rule — but New Yorkers willing to travel an hour are thought to show the commitment needed to take proper care of a dog or cat. Also, there is the occasional listing in the newspaper for free pets, and veterinarian hospitals are also a good place to find postings for free pets.

North Shore Animal League

Address: 25 Davis Avenue, Port Washington, Long Island
Open: Daily, 10:00 am to 9:00 pm
Phone: (516) 883-7575
Comments: Probably Metropolitan New York's only no-fee animal adoption service, this shelter is located in Port Washington, Long Island, roughly a 40 minute car trip from Manhattan. Yet, many New Yorkers still make the drive for kittens, puppies, dogs and cats. An application and screening test are required as are two pieces of picture ID. Most other shelters charge between $50 to $65 per animal, which is not free, but certainly offsets a vet-check.

Veterinary Hospitals

Comments: To find animals free of adoption fees, visiting veterinary hospitals and checking out their bulletin boards is usually productive. And, naturally, classified ads might also yield totally free animals.

Piano Bars

Classic (and free) piano bars are not easy to come by, largely because they're tucked away in a quiet restaurant bar or recessed in pricey hotels, usually unwelcoming to non-guests. While many piano bars can be off-putting and clubby, they are nevertheless open to all. This selection includes piano bars which charge no cover and, with few exceptions, have no drink minimum requirement. However, drink prices at some of these can be alarming to those who think they are enjoying something free. Call ahead and ask for the price range on drinks, so you don't find yourself nursing a tonic water for two hours.

Arthur's Tavern

Address: 57 Grove Street
Open: Sunday and Monday, 8:00 pm to 4:00 am; Tuesday through Saturday, 7:00 pm to 4:00 am
Phone: (212) 675-6879
Comments: Featuring Al Bundy and Sweet Georgia Brown, this Greenwich Village landmark jazz club also has a relaxed neighborhood bar atmosphere earlier in the evenings. A very popular haunt for locals, but watch out for large groups of the Bridge & Tunnel revelers, as well as packs of German-speaking jazz lovers.

Beekman Tower Hotel

Address: First Avenue (at 49th Street)
Open: Live piano music Tuesday through Saturday
Phone: (212) 355-7300
Comments: Piano entertainment at the tony Top of the Tower bar/restaurant each night except Monday, beginning at 9:00 pm (8:00 pm on Sunday). However, there is a $10 drink minimum.

Bemelmans Bar

Address: Carlyle Hotel, Madison Avenue at 76th Street
Phone: (212) 570-7189
Comments: Decorated with murals by childrens books illustrator Ludwig Bemelman (author of the Madelaine books), this pricey Upper East Side establishment has a quiet, elegant atmosphere. It offers a no cover piano bar from around 5:30 until 9:30 pm.

Bill's Gay 90's

Address: 57 East 54th Street
Phone: (212) 355-0243
Comments: Free piano bar Thursday to Sunday, from 8:00 pm to midnight.

Brandy's Piano Bar

Address: 235 East 84th Street (between Second and Third Avenues)
Open: Daily 4:00 pm to 4:00 am. Happy Hour 4:00 pm to 8:30 pm
Phone: (212) 650-1944
Comments: Brandy's offers no cover piano bar each night of the week starting at 9:30 pm. Two drink minimum at a table, no minimum at bar.

Café Pierre

Address: The Pierre Hotel, Fifth Avenue (at 61st Street)
Phone: (212) 940-8195
Comments: Polished landmark in the famed Pierre Hotel with free piano bar. $12 drink minimum every night after 9:30 pm.

Ciel Rouge

Address: 176 Seventh Avenue (between 20th and 21st Streets)
Open: Sunday through Thursday, 7:00 pm to 2:00 am; Friday and Saturday, 7:00 pm to 3:00 am
Phone: (212) 929-5542
Comments: Tucked away in Chelsea without any sign outside, Ciel Rouge is one of the city's most unique and hard-to-notice haunts. Inside, with almost everything decked out in red, it makes for one of the most peculiar and pleasing piano bars. No cover and no drink minimum. Piano usually starts around 9:00 pm.

Danny's Skylight Room at the Grand Sea Palace

Address: 346 West 46th Street (between Eighth and Ninth Avenues)
Phone: (212) 265-8133
Comments: Theater district restaurant bar with no cover piano bar 8:00 pm to midnight.

Don't Tell Mama

Address: 343 West 46th Street (between Eighth and Ninth Avenues)
Open: Daily 4:00 pm to 4:00 am
Phone: (212) 757-0788
Comments: A sometimes raucous and packed piano bar in the heart of the theater district. No cover piano plus singing daily from 9:00 pm to around 3:00 am. Two drink minimum if you take a table.

Duplex Cabaret/Piano Bar/Cafe

Address: 61 Christopher Street (off Seventh Avenue)
Phone: (212) 255-5438
Comments: Each night beginning at 9:00 pm, Duplex Piano bar entertains until the early hours of the morning with show tunes and jazz. Two drink minimum at table, none at bar. No cover.

Eighty-Eight's

Address: 228 West 10th Street (between Hudson and Bleeker)
Phone: (212) 924-0088
Comments: Popular Greenwich Village sing-along piano bar. No cover, but there is a two drink minimum.

Halcyon

Address: 151 West 54th Street
Open: Tuesday through Saturday, 8:00 pm through midnight
Phone: (212) 468-8888
Comments: Upscale, quiet lounge with no cover piano bar in elegant surroundings. Piano playing Tuesday through Saturday, 4:00 pm to 8:00 pm.

Harry's Bar

Address: 212 East 42nd Street
Phone: (212) 490-8900
Comments: Piano music for no cover or minimum nightly from 5:00 pm to 8:00 pm weekdays at Harry's Bar, the elegant watering hole at the Helmsley Hotel.

Hors d'Oeuvres (also known as The Greatest Bar on Earth)

Address: 1 World Trade Center, 107th floor
Phone: (212) 938-1111
Comments: A piano bar without cover starting at 4:00 pm with panoramic views of the city and surrounding area in the heart of the financial district. $5 cover Thursday through Saturday after 9:00 pm.

Le Parker Meridian Hotel

Address: 199 West 56th Street
Open: Music free Monday through Saturday beginning 6:00 pm
Phone: (212) 245-5000
Comments: Free piano bar and live entertainment after 6:00 pm, Monday through Saturday in Le Parker's French-style bar/restaurant, Bar Montparnasse. Due to reopen in April, 1998.

Liberty Lounge, New York Marriott Financial Center

Address: 85 West Street
Phone: (212) 385-4900
Comments: Elegant moderately-priced bar with Wall Street theme. And steady piano accompaniment on Saturday evenings.

Lobby Court Lounge,
Sheraton New York Hotel & Towers

Address: 811 Seventh Avenue
Phone: (212) 581-1000
Comments: This elegant lounge features Irving Fields on the piano playing a classic repertoire nearly every night.

Oak Room, The Plaza Hotel

Address: 768 Fifth Avenue (at 59th Street)
Phone: (212) 759-3000
Comments: A classic New York landmark, this pricey establishment features piano almost every night.

Oaks Piano Bar and Restaurant, The

Address: 49 Grove Street
Phone: (212) 367-9390
Open: Daily 5:00 pm to 4:00 am
Comments: A usually packed Greenwich Village piano bar belting out

show tunes nightly from 6:00 pm to 4:00 am, without cover or minimum drink requirement.

Regents

Address: 317 East 53rd Street (between First and Second Avenue)
Phone: (212) 593-3091
Comments: Theater district piano bar without cover or minimum drink requirement. On weekdays, music begins at 8:00 pm and continues to midnight. On Saturday, music starts at 8:30 pm.

Rose's Turn

Address: 55 Grove Street
Phone: (212) 366-5438
Comments: Greenwich Village piano bar specializing in show tunes and featuring a wait and bartending staff appropriately smitten with the songs and spirit of Broadway.

UN Plaza-Park Hyatt

Address: One United Nations Plaza (at East 44th Street and First Avenue)
Open: 5:30 pm to 1:00 am
Phone: (212) 702-5014
Comments: The piano bar in the Ambassador Lounge at the UN Plaza-Park Hyatt offers music nightly from 7:00 pm to 12:00 pm without cover or drink minimum requirement. A dark, romantic and elegant lounge.

Waldorf-Astoria Hotel

Address: Park Avenue and 50th Street
Phone: (212) 355-3000
Comments: No cover, no minimum drink requirement at the famed Waldorf-Astoria's opulent lounge, the Cocktail Terrace. Music playing from 4:00 pm to 9:00 pm.

Places for Children

There are lots of places to bring children in New York in nice weather: Central Park, Rockefeller Center, Times Square, etc. But sometimes these spots end up burdening parents with constant appeals for needless trinkets, or are too crowded to leisurely appreciate with toddlers. Below is a list of spots geared toward children, most of which are indoors. They are used to catering to children's needs, or even entertaining and educating them for hours.

Alley Pond Environmental Center

Address: 228-06 Northern Boulevard, Douglastown, Queens
Open: Tuesday through Friday, 9:00 am to 4:30 pm; Saturday, 9:30 am to 3:30 pm
Phone: (718) 229-4000
Comments: Including some 150 acres of wetlands, this center serves primarily as an educational center. It has trails for children as well as an aquarium and a small animal room.

Belvedere Castle

Address: Central Park, near 79th Street and south of the Great Lawn.
Open: Visitor's Center open Tuesday through Sunday, 11:00 am to 5:00 pm
Phone: (212) 772-0210
Comments: A hub of Central Park, and a great place to bring children, the medieval-design castle is an education center for adults and especially children, sponsoring nature exhibits on geology, park history and wildlife as well as many types of entertainment. It is the base for the city's Urban Park Rangers and is also New York's National Weather Service Station.

Brooklyn Children's Museum

Address: 145 Brooklyn Avenue (at St. Marks Avenue), Brooklyn
Open: During academic year: Monday, Wednesday, Thursday and Friday, 2:00 pm to 5:00 pm; Saturday and school holidays, 10:00 am to 5:00 pm. Summer hours: 10:00 am to 5:00 pm, each day except Tuesday.
Phone: (718) 735-4400

Comments: Billed as the world's first children's museum, The Brooklyn Children's Museum has been a popular attraction since it opened its doors in 1899. Exhibitions are drawn from the museum's some 20,000 items and are aimed at educating children with cultural, historical and scientific lessons in a hands-on, creative and fun fashion. Charges $3 suggested admission, but pay what you can policy is acceptable, if necessary.

Bureau of Day Care

Address: 65 Worth Street, 4th floor
Phone: (212) 676-2444
Comments: This agency, run by the New York City Department of Health, is charged with licensing day care facilities in the city's boroughs. It also offers suggestions and consultation on day care centers in any given neighborhood. Call for advice and ask for the comprehensive lists it offers.

Charles A. Dana Discovery Center

Address: 36 West 110th Street (at Fifth Avenue)
Open: Tuesday through Sunday, 11:00 am to 5:00 pm
Phone: (212) 860-1370
Comments: Family workshops offered on weekends. Harlem Meer Performance Festival held every Saturday afternoon from May to August. Also provides fishing rods and bait, rental-free, for fishing in the nearby Harlem Meer lake. Houses "The Fragile Forest," an exhibition on the ecosystem of the forest.

Children's Museum of the Arts

Address: 72 Spring Street (between Broadway and Lafayette Street)
Open: Tuesday through Sunday, 11:00 am to 5:00 pm; Thursday 11:00 am to 7:00 pm. Free of charge Thursday, 4:00 pm to 7:00 pm only.
Phone: (212) 941-9198
Comments: Museum featuring artwork aimed at piquing children's interest in different art forms. Arts programs and interactive exhibitions for children 18 months to 10 years of age are aimed at fostering positive interaction and self-confidence. While there is a modest admission charge, that fee sometimes covers free workshops, performances and special events. Plans to find a new home in 1998, so call for new address.

Children's Museum of Manhattan

Address: The Tisch Building, 212 West 83rd Street
Open: Wednesday through Sunday, 10:00 am to 5:00 pm
Phone: (212) 721-1234
Comments: Designed for children ages 2 through 10, includes a culturally diverse environment through interactive, hands-on exhibitions, education and outreach programs. Children under one year of age are admitted free; suggested donation of $5 for others, but paying what you wish is acceptable.

Fraunces Tavern Museum

Address: 54 Pearl Street
Open: Monday through Saturday, 10:00 am to 4:45 pm; Saturday and Sunday, Noon to 4:00 pm
Phone: (212) 425-1778
Comments: Built in 1719, Wall Street's Fraunces Tavern is one of the city's most treasured landmarks, largely because of George Washington's associations with the building. Permanent exhibition includes impressive collection of Revolutionary War era paintings and articles. The museum is free for children six and under. But for others, the museum hosts a string of special Thursday evening historical lectures which are free with the $2.50 admission. Also notable are the "Family Saturdays," held once a month, offering revolutionary theme programs (like Mask Making Colonial Craft Day) usually held from noon to 4:00 pm.

Greenwich Village Youth Council

Address: 25 Carmine Street
Phone: (212) 242-2743
Comments: Dedicated to improving the educational and cultural lives of teenagers in the Greenwich Village community. Offers cultural events, counseling, recreational activities and referrals. Call for details on free services and activities.

Hans Christian Andersen Statue

Address: Central Park, near 72nd Street entrance on the east side of Park
Open: Generally during summer
Comments: Storytellers meet to share their craft with old and young alike at this apt spot in Central Park daily at 11:00 am during warm months.

Ottendorfer Library

Address: 135 Second Avenue
Phone: (212) 674-0947
Comments: Classic children's films for free on Saturdays at 2:00 pm.

Sony Wonder Technology Lab

Address: 550 Madison Avenue (between 55th and 56th Streets)
Open: Tuesday through Friday, 10:00 am to 6:00 pm; Sunday, Noon to 6:00 pm
Phone: (212) 833-8100
Comments: More of a playground for technology enthusiasts than a museum, the "Lab" is full of interactive and entertaining gadgets and tools for learning the basics of technology. Four stories of multi-media hands-on gadgets and displays. A popular stop for children as well as for adults.

Staten Island Children's Museum

Address: Sung Harbor, 1000 Richmond Terrace, Staten Island
Open: Tuesday through Sunday, Noon to 5:00 pm
Phone: (718) 273-2060
Comments: Located at Snug Harbor, this museum features a fantasy frigate and an oversized anthill for children to interact with. Also, workshops and performances are offered to expand children's imagination and knowledge base. Children under 2 years of age admitted free of charge; others are suggested to contribute $4.

Publications

There are scores of free local papers in the city's boroughs. The free publications listed below are those that will most likely yield useful information in the way of events listings and services.

Downtown Express
Comments: A bi-weekly newspaper covering south of TriBeCa with news, features, and a calendar of events.

lgny
Address: 150 Fifth Avenue, 6th floor
Phone: (212) 691-1100
Comments: A free lesbian and gay weekly newspaper at kiosks as well as vendor boxes on street corners.

New York Press
Address: 295 Lafayette
Phone: (212) 244-2282
Comments: Includes excellent events listings and restaurant information and reviews.

News Communications, Inc.
Address: 242 West 30th Street
Phone: (212) 268-8600
Comments: News Communications publishes the following local newspapers, all of which have calendar of events listings and news: *Our Town* (Upper East Side); *Manhattan Spirit* (Upper West Side); *Queen's Tribune* (Queens); *Brooklyn Skyliner* (Brooklyn); and *Bronx Press Review* (Bronx).

Village Voice

Address: 36 Cooper Square
Phone: (212) 475-3300
Comments: A mainstay leftist weekly in New York for events, club listings, real estate and personal classifieds, as well as features. Found at most newsstands. Hits stands Tuesday nights. Not free outside Manhattan.

Religious Buildings

New York possesses some of the country's oldest and most spectacular churches, cathedrals, synagogues and other houses of worship. And, as in any major city, many of them have become standard tourist attractions. Apart from being striking architectural rarities, the religious buildings selected here also serve as vitalizing spots for rest and reflection. Most also offer choral and organ music, as well as cultural events (covered in other chapters of this book).

Cathedral Church of St. John the Divine

Address: Amsterdam Avenue and 112th Street
Open: Open every day, 7:00 am to 5:00 pm. The stoneyard is open Monday through Friday, 9:00 am to 5:00 pm
Phone: (212) 316-7540
Comments: With construction begun in 1892, and still only about two-thirds complete, this Gothic cathedral is already the world's largest. Stonecutters are still at work, and their stone yard is open for visitation. Known also for its choral vespers, choral Eucharists and organ meditations.

Eldridge Street Synagogue

Address: 12 Eldridge Street (between Canal and Division Streets)
Open: Monday through Friday, 10:00 am to 6:00 pm
Phone: (212) 219-0888
Comments: Located in the Lower East Side, home to many Jewish immigrants over the decades since it was built in 1887. The synagogue, in its elegant Moorish style with 70-foot ceilings, sponsors changing exhibitions focusing on the Jewish experience. A past show: "Welcome to America," a mixed media presentation described the lives of Eastern European women. Call for an appointment to see occasional exhibitions, book signings, lectures and holiday programs, and to find out which events are free and open to the public.

Islamic Cultural Center

Address: 1711 Third Avenue (at East 96th Street)
Phone: (212) 722-5234
Comments: One of the city's first mosques, it serves as a focus for the

Upper East Side's Muslim residents.

Riverside Church

Address: 490 Riverside Drive (between 120th and 122nd Streets)
Open: 9:00 am to 6:00 pm
Phone: (212) 870-6700
Comments: Known for its 400-foot tower with 74 bells inside, representing the largest such grouping in the world. Tours free for groups, but call ahead to make arrangements.

St. Bartholomew's Church

Address: Park Avenue at 51st Street
Open: 7:30 am to 6:30 pm
Phone: (212) 378-0200
Comments: A particularly beautiful historic church in Byzantine style. Apart from regular services, this church hosts many family, cultural and musical events open to the public, most free of charge.

St. Patrick's Cathedral

Address: Fifth Avenue (at 50th Street)
Open: Open seven days, 7:00 am to 8:45 pm
Phone: (212) 753-2261
Comments: New York's most well known house of worship, St. Patrick's is also one the country's most impressive examples of Gothic architecture. Built in 1888, with a 26-foot diameter rose window, organ with 9,000 pipes and height of 330 feet from ground level to top of tower. Organ recitals on some Sundays, plus concert series. Call for details.

Temple Emanu-El

Address: Fifth Avenue at 65th Street
Phone: (212) 744-1400
Comments: The city's biggest synagogue, it possesses Byzantine and Near Eastern motifs.

Trinity Church

Address: Corner of Wall Street and Broadway
Open: Church is open from Monday to Friday, 7:00 am to 6:00 pm; Sunday; 12:30 pm to 4:00 pm. Concerts every Thursday at 1:00 pm
Phone: (212) 602-0747
Comments: A needed respite for weary Wall Streeters, and popular stop for tourists at one of the city's oldest and historic churches.

Resources for the Disabled

For disabled New Yorkers, and especially disabled tourists, this city can be extremely difficult to navigate. This chapter includes a few dependable sources of information and groups, which make living in and visiting New York much easier for those with particular needs.

Access for All
Phone: (212) 575-7663
Comments: An exhaustive guidebook on events and cultural goings-on accessible to the disabled which can be obtained free of charge by writing to: Hospital Audiences, 220 West 42nd Street, New York, NY 10036, or by calling the above number.

Big Apple Greeters
Address: 1 Center Street
Phone: (212) 669-3602
Comments: A free public service, Big Apple Greeters is dedicated to assisting the disabled tourist see the city with a volunteer guide free of charge. The service matches visitors with New Yorker volunteer guides with similar interests (and languages). Also provides other services for the disabled traveler in New York. Call and ask for a request form. Appointments are usually filled within three days of receiving the request. Or, drop by their office and fill out a request.

Lighthouse, The
Address: 11 East 59th Street
Phone: (212) 821-9200
Comments: Holds art installations meant to be felt, not seen, for the blind or visually impaired. Provides Braille literature and other services for the blind. In the past, shows included "Styrofoam Installation #2," a "tactile" installation by Sol LeWitt.

Mayor's Office for People with Disabilities, The
Address: 52 Chambers Street
Phone: (212) 788-2830
Comments: Exhaustive information on accessibility around the city for disabled people.

New York Society for the Deaf

Address: 817 Broadway

Phone: (212) 777-3900

Comments: A rich source for services and contacts to groups which serve the deaf.

Restful Places

There are peaceful havens in New York for weary travelers and spent city dwellers. These places offer respite to those who need to be away from the noise of traffic, the nagging of panhandlers and the incessant spending. They are mostly indoor public spots designed to provide comfort in the stultifying heat or bitter cold. They also can be places to eat a bag lunch or relax with a newspaper. Parks, in fine weather, fit this bill, but are listed in their own category in this book.

American Academy of Arts and Letters, Audubon Terrace
Address: Broadway and 155th Street
Phone: (212) 368-5900
Comments: The Audubon Terrace affords a tranquil setting in a quiet, formal atmosphere. In the same building are other peaceful spots: Hispanic Society of America and the American Numismatic Society.

Citicorp Center Public Atrium
Address: East 53rd Street at Lexington Avenue
Phone: (212) 559-6758
Comments: A great place to rest and take in special seasonal exhibitions. Also, look out for the annual model train display, shown during the winter holidays.

Equitable Tower Atrium
Address: 787 Seventh Avenue (between 51st and 52nd Streets)
Comments: An open space for weary mid-towners and tourists, alike. A good place for visitors to rest and regroup.

Ford Foundation Building
Address: 230 East 43rd Street (between First and Second Avenues)
Phone: (212) 573-5000
Comments: A beautiful atrium area, welcome to the public for those seeking peace.

Madison Sculpture Garden

Address: Fifth Avenue (between 56th and 57th Streets)
Comments: Serene garden populated with pieces of sculpture.

New York Earth Room

Address: 141 Wooster Street
Comments: A room filled with soil yielding a sense of bucolic calm (and aroma). One of New York's most intriguing and restful spots.

Open Center Meditation Room

Address: Broadway and Crosby
Open: Monday through Friday, 10:00 am to 10:00 pm; Saturday, 9:00 am to 10:00 pm; Sunday, 9:00 am to 6:00 pm
Phone: (212) 219-2527
Comments: Free to public, the center offers spaces for meditation and reflection with visitors respecting the quiet of others.

St. Paul's Churchyard

Address: Broadway between Fulton and Vesey Streets
Phone: (212) 602-0874
Comments: A sister church of Trinity Church, St. Paul's also has a placid graveyard amidst the frenetic Wall Street area. Buried there are: revolutionary war hero General Richard Montgomery and renown early 19th century actor George Frederick Cooke.

Terrace at Blue Cross Center, The

Address: 622 Third Avenue (at 40th Street)
Comments: A peaceful mid-town enclave away from the city's din.

Trinity Church Graveyard

Address: Corner of Wall Street and Broadway
Phone: (212) 602-0747
Comments: In back of Wall Street's venerated landmark is one of Downtown's most tranquil places. Opened in 1703, the graveyard, dwarfed by Wall Street's towers, offers benches for visitors to the burial sites of some of early New York's most prominent figures, including Alexander Hamilton and Robert Fulton.

United Nations Garden

Address: First Avenue (at 45th Street)

Comments: A popular large garden near the UN, and the East River.

Water Street Plaza
Address: 55 Water Street (at Old Slip Road)
Comments: A good place to rest your feet after traipsing around Wall Street. Also next to South Street Seaport.

Winter Garden, World Financial Center
Address: On Hudson River at north end of Liberty Street.
Comments: The World Financial Center's Winter Garden, a colossal three-story atrium with a new set of towering palm trees lined in colonnades, also throws regular concerts usually scheduled for 6:00 pm. A great contemplative place to read, sip coffee or have quiet conversation. When weather permits, concerts and performances held outside Winter Garden in surrounding plazas.

Societies & Institutes

New York is home to numerous institutes and societies dedicated to almost every imaginable interest or cause. While many are focused primarily on scholarship and study, most open their doors to the uninitiated through lectures, and artistic and cultural events.

American-Irish Historical Society

Address: 991 Fifth Avenue (at 80th Street)
Open: Monday through Friday, 10:30 am to 5:00 pm. Be sure to ring the doorbell to get in.
Phone: (212) 288-2263
Comments: Dedicated to history and tradition of American-Irish relations, this Society offers exhibitions on Irish-American figures and affairs. The building housing the Society, built in 1900, is also of historical significance. Also has research library and archives.

American Numismatic Society

Address: Broadway at West 155th Street (between 155th and 156th Streets)
Open: Tuesday through Saturday, 9:00 am to 4:30 pm; Sunday, 1:00 pm to 4:00 pm.
Phone: (212) 234-3130
Comments: (see Museums)

Americas Society& Council of the Americas

Address: 680 Park Avenue (at 68th Street)
Phone: (212) 249-8950
Comments: Devoted to preserving and promulgating the intellectual and cultural history of the Americas, this Society holds many free lectures and changing exhibitions. Past lectures included "The Genesis of the Text: Translating Latin American Literature," which explored the translation of important contemporary and past works of Latin writers.

Asia Society

Address: 725 Park Avenue (at 70th Street)
Open: Tuesday, Wednesday, Friday and Saturday, 10:00 am to 6:00

pm; Thursday, 11:00 am to 8:00 pm; Sunday, Noon to 5:00 pm. Free on Thursdays, 6:00 pm to 8:00 pm

Phone: Events information: (212) 517-NEWS; General information: (212) 288-6400

Comments: Hosts a vibrant program, including lectures, musical dance performances as well as changing exhibitions, most of which are fee-based and related to Asian history and culture. However, the society does open its doors free to the public on Thursdays, 6:00 pm to 8:00 pm. Call for free events and gallery exhibitions.

Bible House

Address: 1865 Broadway (at 61st Street) 12th floor

Open: Monday through Friday, 9:00 am to 4:30 pm

Phone: (212) 408-1200

Comments: Home to the American Bible Society, the Bible House is a broad collection of rare and unique bibles. Hosts exhibitions in its gallery focusing on Bible themes and history. Houses some 50,000 articles related to Scripture, as well as photographs, recordings and correspondence.

Czech Center

Address: 1109 Madison Avenue (at 83rd Street)

Open: Tuesday through Friday, 9:00 am to 5:00 pm

Phone: (212) 288-0830

Comments: Dedicated to promulgating Czech history and culture, the Center offers frequent exhibitions and lectures. Past exhibitions included "Vaclav Havel: Dissident/President," a photographic history of the Czech Republic's famed leader.

Fashion Institute of Technology Gallery

Address: Seventh Avenue (at West 27th Street)

Open: Tuesday, 10:00 am through 9:00 pm; Wednesday through Saturday; 10:00 am through 5:00 pm

Phone: (212) 217-7999

Comments: Housed in the Fashion Institute of Technology, a hub for the nation's budding fashion designers, the gallery features rolling exhibits in its Shirley Goodman Resource Center.

Goethe House New York

Address: 1014 Fifth Avenue (at 82nd Street)

Open: Tuesday and Thursday, 9:00 am to 5:00 pm; Wednesday and

Friday, 9:00 am to 5:00 pm; Saturday, Noon to 5:00 pm (gallery and library hours apply year-round except for summer, when it is closed)
Phone: (212) 439-8700
Comments: This New York arm of the Goethe Institute based in Munich offers what is standard in other branches: changing exhibitions, various cultural events, lectures, films and language instruction (for fee) as well as an extensive library containing some 16,000 German language books, periodicals and recordings.

Hebrew Union College – Jewish Institute of Religion
Address: Brookdale Center, 1 West 4th Street (between Broadway and Mercer)
Phone: (212) 674-5300
Comments: This Institute offers frequent art exhibitions and lectures to the public free of charge, not necessarily directly related to Judaica.

Hispanic Society of America, The
Address: Broadway at 15th Street
Open: Tuesday through Saturday, 10:00 am to 4:30 pm; Sunday, 1:00 pm to 4:30 pm
Phone: (212) 690-0743
Comments: Dedicated to Spanish and Portuguese history and culture and founded in 1904, the Society houses a collection that includes ancient fragments from Roman settlements in Spain, decorative arts from prehistory to current, as well as tens of thousands of books and manuscripts on Hispanic historical themes. Also houses an iconography collection, globes, prints and other matter.

Horticultural Society of New York
Address: 128 West 58th Street
Phone: (212) 757-0915
Comments: Home of the Horticulture Resource Center, the society houses a research library as well as a greenhouse, shop and education program. Call for free events.

Institute for Art and Urban Resources
Address: 46-01 21st Street, Long Island City, Queens
Open: Open November through May; Wednesday through Sunday, Noon to 6:00 pm
Phone: (718) 784-2084
Comments: A local arts and cultural center, the Institute, a reconstructed

public school, hosts an array of painting and other visual arts exhibitions as well as dramatic works.

Japan House

Address: 333 East 47th Street
Open: Tuesday through Sunday, 11:00 am to 5:00 pm
Phone: (212) 832-1155
Comments: Home to the Japan Society, The Japan House sponsors changing exhibitions and lectures germane to Japan and Japan-American relations. A recent free exhibition was "Japanese Theater in the World," highlighting masks, and costumes from 1,500 years of Japanese theater arts.

Mechanics and Tradesmens Institute and The John M. Mossman Collection of Locks

Address: 20 West 44th Street
Open: Monday through Friday, 10:00 am to Noon; 1:00 pm to 4:00 pm
Phone: (212) 840-1840
Comments: Formerly a trade school, the institute is now open free to the public. Included is a library with an eclectic assortment of books; of greater interest is the lock museum with hundreds of examples of locks through the ages.

Municipal Art Society

Address: Urban Center, 457 Madison Avenue (at 51st Street)
Open: Monday through Wednesday, Friday and Saturday, 11:00 am to 5:00 pm
Phone: (212) 935-3960
Comments: Geared toward promoting urban design and renewal, the Society sponsors many free exhibitions and lectures.

New York Academy of Medicine

Address: 1216 Fifth Avenue (at 103rd Street)
Phone: (212) 822-7200 (extension 7321)
Comments: A professional group first, the academy organizes exhibitions on medicine. Past displays included "A Perpetual Fever Nest: Epidemics in 19th Century New York," an exploration of the diseases and cures in 19th century New York.

New York City Audubon Society

Address: 71 West 23rd Street
Open: Monday through Friday, 10:00 am to 4:00 pm
Phone: (212) 691-7483
Comments: Presents periodic lectures on birds and birding. Also sponsors outings, but most for a modest fee. Call for details.

New York Historical Society

Address: 170 Central Park West
Open: Monday through Friday, 10:00 am to 4:00 pm
Phone: (212) 873-3400
Comments: Houses a research library, fine original Audubon watercolors as well as a solid collection of books and other material on the city's history. Lectures and special events, some free of charge.

PEN American Center

Address: 568 Broadway (between Prince and Houston Streets)
Open: Monday through Friday, 9:30 am to 5:30 pm
Phone: (212) 334-1660
Comments: This international group is dedicated to supporting the artistic freedom and achievements of writers throughout the world. The center sponsors many free lectures and readings on myriad topics. Past series included, the "World-in-Translation Month" which highlighted important translations of writers with readings and panel discussions.

Queens Historical Society

Address: 143-35 37th Avenue, Flushing, Queens
Phone: (718) 939-0647
Comments: Free information to take a self-guided tour through Flushing.

Society of Illustrators

Address: 128 East 63rd Street (at Lexington Avenue)
Open: Tuesday, 10:00 am to 8:00 pm; Wednesday through Friday, 10:00 am to 5:00 pm; Saturday, Noon to 4:00 pm
Phone: (212) 838-2560
Comments: Houses changing exhibitions in its two galleries, mostly on commercial art by artists well regarded outside the advertising realm, such as Norman Rockwell. The society's permanent collection, which numbers over 2,000 pieces, is also represented by a few hundred selections on display.

Schomberg Center for Research in Black Culture

Address: 515 Lenox Avenue (at 135th Street)

Open. Monday through Wednesday, Noon to 8:00 pm; Thursday through Saturday, 10:00 am to 6:00 pm. Summer hours may vary.

Phone: (212) 491-2000

Comments: Dedicated to the study of the history and culture of peoples of African origin, this Center offers a wealth of resources with over five million items including: about 150,000 volumes, 300,000 photos and other documents. Routinely holds exhibitions; and lectures. Past exhibitions included: "America's Reconstruction: People and Politics After the Civil War."

Spanish Institute, The; Center for American-Spanish Affairs

Address: 684 Park Avenue (at 68th Street)

Open: Exhibition hours: Monday through Saturday, 11:00 am to 5:00 pm

Phone: (212) 628-0420

Comments: Changing exhibitions including prominent contemporary artists. Also sponsors lectures on Spanish cultural, political and artistic affairs.

Swiss Institute

Address: 495 Broadway (between Broome and Spring Streets)

Phone: (212) 925-2035

Comments: Dedicated to promoting the cultural and international achievements of Switzerland. The Swiss Institute distinguishes itself with its full program of free events, including films, exhibitions, readings, lectures and concerts. Most events center on Swiss or Swiss-American figures or themes.

Ukrainian Institute of America

Address: 2 East 79th Street

Open: Tuesday through Friday, 2:00 pm to 6:00 pm

Phone: (212) 288-8660

Comments: Exhibited in this grand mansion are artworks and crafts – both modern and traditional – representative of Ukrainian culture and tradition. Also concerts and shows, mostly for a charge.

Van Allen Institute

Address: 30 West 22nd Street (between Fifth and Sixth Avenues)
Phone: (212) 924-7000
Comments: Dedicated to art and architecture, the Institute opens its doors to the public for special exhibitions. Past shows included "The New River Project Exhibition," which highlighted building plans for restoration of the Hudson River.

YIVO Institute For Jewish Research

Address: 1048 Fifth Avenue (at 86th Street)
Open: Monday through Thursday, 9:30 am to 5:30 pm
Phone: (212) 246-6080
Comments: The YIVO is an important repository for modern Judaica including: about 1,000 photographs, 300,000 books and over 20 million other various documents relating to the history of Eastern European Jews. Many articles in the collection had been preserved through the Holocaust. The YIVO holds exhibitions on the history and culture of Eastern European and American Jewry.

Theater

With Broadway tickets astronomical even at half price through TKS kiosks, it is often quite difficult to find any decent plays for under $20. This list should guide you to some of the city's free theater, from raw to refined. Also, check out off-Broadway and community theaters for occasional free readings or rehearsals.

78th Street Theater Lab

Address: 236 West 78th Street, 2nd floor
Phone: (212) 873-9050
Comments: Occasionally holds free readings and stagings of new plays and standard classics.

Actors Studio

Address: 432 West 44th Street (between Ninth & Tenth Avenues)
Open: 9:00 am to 5:00 pm, Monday though Friday by appointment only; tickets are available from the International Theatre Institute (212-254-4141)
Phone: (212) 757-0870
Comments: Produces free plays from the Fall into Spring. Call for production schedule and confirm no-charge events.

Broadway on Broadway

Address: Times Square, Broadway and Seventh Avenues between 43rd and 48th Streets
Phone: (212) 768-1560
Comments: Broadway stars take to Times Square annually in early September for a free performance of song and dance from major current Broadway hits.

Free Theater Project

Address: 311 West 80th Street
Comments: The Free Theater Project sponsors free performances monthly at noon by well-noted actors and actresses. Call for details on who is slated and when.

Gene Frankel Theater & Workshop

Address: 24 Bond Street
Phone: (212) 777-1767
Comments: This venerable East Village theater laboratory opens its doors to the public for free on occasion for performances and studies, as well as readings. Call for details.

Juilliard School

Address: 144 West 66th Street
Open: September through June
Phone: (212) 799-5000
Comments: Drawn from Juilliard's Drama Division, some of the nation's most promising drama students present plays at the school's Drama Theater, located at Lincoln Center. Free performances on occasion. Call for details, or subscribe to the school's mailing list, including many drama events as well as music and dance.

New Dramatists

Address: 424 West 44th Street
Phone: (212) 757-6960
Comments: For decades, this theater has fostered emerging playwrights and budding actors. Performances are generally free, but tickets may be challenging to secure. Call ahead.

Shakespeare in the Park

Address: Delacorte Theater, Central Park West at 81st Street
Phone: (212) 861-7277
Comments: Sponsored by The New York Shakespeare festival (212-539-8500), and renown as Joseph Papp's brainchild, this annual summer event has become a fixture in Central Park and for theatergoers. Look out for listings, or call for details. Tickets are free, but are distributed on the day of the show, and are typically obtained after a long wait in line.

Shakespeare in the Parking Lot

Address: 85 Ludlow Street
Comments: A glib but impressive answer to Shakespeare in the Park, this summer series presents Shakespeare's works to the public free of charge in fresh, innovative productions.

St. Mark's-in-the-Bowery

Address: 131 East 10th Street (at Second Avenue)
Open: 10:00 am to 6:00 pm, Monday through Friday
Phone: (212) 674-8194
Comments: Home to a broad range of artistic and cultural events, many free of charge. Occasionally free theater performances, poetry readings and dance performances. Call events reservations for information, and (212) 674-0910 for poetry readings; (212) 674-8112 for dance performances.

Theaterworks/USA

Address: Promenade Theater, 2162 Broadway (at 72nd Street)
Phone: (212) 647-1100
Comments: Theaterworks/USA, based in the Promenade Theater, opens its doors to the public for free performances throughout the summer. A popular spot to bring children. Call for details.

West Bank Café

Address: 407 West 42nd Street
Phone: (212) 695-6909
Comments: A landmark theater district congregation for theater people, the West Bank Café also houses the Downstairs Theater Bar, where experimental and new works are often first glimpsed. Call for free performances or open mikes.

Tours

Not only tourists take tours in New York. And not all tours come with a fee attached. There are some delightful tours offered regularly, mostly sponsored by community development groups. These are aimed at acquainting visitors and New Yorkers with certain areas in order to draw business and pedestrian activity to those neighborhoods. This doesn't mean they are any less interesting than their many counterparts which can charge up to $40. Most hubs in Manhattan are represented — The Wall Street District, 42nd Street, the Empire State Building area, and Harlem. For those who hate tours, or don't have the time to catch one, there is a lot of free material available for the self-guided tourist.

34th Street Tours

Address: 32nd Street and Seventh Avenue
Open: Thursdays, 12:30 pm
Phone: (212) 868-0521
Comments: This group offers free tours on Thursdays at 12:30 pm that focus on the history and architecture of the Empire State Building area. Meets at Empire State Building entrance. Also offers free Penn Station tours on the last Monday of each month at noon at the information booth in the main concourse.

American Stock Exchange

Address: 86 Trinity Place
Phone: (212) 306-1000
Comments: Free tours of this financial market nerve center. Call for reservations.

Battery Park City Gardens Horticultural Tours

Address: Rector Gate, Battery Park City
Phone: (212) 267-9700
Comments: Hosts free weekly tours throughout the summer. Tour guides begin walks through the Battery Park gardens at 12:30 pm and 6:00 pm on Thursdays at Rector Gate, located at the south end of Rector Street in Battery Park City. Held May through June. Call for details.

Big Apple Greeters

Address: 1 Center Street
Phone: (212) 669-3602
Comments: A free public service, Big Apple Greeters is dedicated to assisting tourists see the city with a volunteer guide free of charge. The service matches visitors with New Yorker volunteer guides (with similar interests and languages). Call and ask for a request form. Appointments are usually filled within three days of receiving the request. Or, drop by their office and fill out a request.

City Hall

Address: Broadway and Murray Streets
Phone: (212) 788-7585
Comments: A popular stop for tourists, free tours offer a glimpse into the mayor's milieu. Portraits, antique furniture and inspiring architecture make this a worthy visit. Also holds changing exhibits on art and history.

Columbia University

Address: The campus is described by Broadway and Amsterdam Avenue and West 114th and 120th Streets
Open: Tours usually offered September through May, Monday through Friday, 11:00 pm and 2:00 pm. During the summer months – May through August, hours vary.
Phone: (212) 854-4900
Comments: Tours are offered, but calling beforehand is suggested to ensure that tours are taking place, and whether non-prospective students are welcome. Schedule varies from semester to semester. Meet at the Visitor's Center, 116th and Broadway at the Low Memorial Library, Room 213.

Commodities Exchange Center

Address: 4 World Trade Center
Phone: (212) 748-3000
Comments: Features a Visitors Gallery for a peek at the most raucous trading activity in New York.

Federal Reserve Bank of New York

Address: 33 Liberty Street (between William & Nassau Streets)
Phone: (212) 720-6130
Comments: By appointment only. Free, one-hour tours through the

bank must be arranged at least one week in advance. Tickets are sent by mail.

Gracie Mansion

Address: East 88th Street & East End Avenue, in Carl Schurz Park
Open: Wednesday, 10:00 am, 11:00 am, 1:00 pm, and 2:00 pm for guided tours
Phone: (212) 570-4751
Comments: Home of the City's mayor. Reservations are accepted from mid-March to mid-November. Suggested donation is $4, but is not technically required.

New York Stock Exchange

Address: 20 Broad Street
Open: Open Monday through Friday, 9:00 am to 4:30 pm
Phone: (212) 656-5165
Comments: A fascinating view above the trading floor of the world's most important stock exchange. Visitors line up in droves daily to see the activity. Also offers a thorough historical perspective on the NYSE. Arrive at the Exchange at about 8:45 am to get free tickets or earlier, for lines typically lengthen quickly.

NYC Tours

Address: 1234 Fifth Avenue, 1st floor
Open: Public tours have been held on Saturdays and Sundays
Phone: 1-800-201-7275
Comments: Free nature walk tours in the Central Park area. Call for details on when tours are given and meeting places. Tours are occasional and center on environmental education and the history of Central Park and are organized by the city's respected Urban Park Rangers.

Orchard Street Shopping District Tour

Address: Tours meet at Katz's Deli, 205 East Houston Street at Ludlow Street
Open: Sunday, 11:00 am
Phone: (212) 226-9010
Comments: Designed to familiarize visitors with the often confusing and sometimes daunting Lower East Side which, when understood, can yield impressive deals. Sponsored by the Lower East Side Business Improvement District. March to December.

Rockefeller Center

Address: 1230 Avenue of the Americas
Phone: (212) 632-3975
Comments: Free guide maps for self-guided tours are offered at Rockefeller Center, a 19-building complex including such American media giants and companies as the Associated Press and Simon & Schuster and NBC. Foyers of many of these buildings include rare works of art. Also, the Center includes parks, gardens and the outdoor skating rink, a popular attraction for tourists and New Yorkers alike. Get brochures at the General Electric building lobby from 8:00 am to 6:00 pm every day of the year.

The Grand Tour

Address: Corner of 42nd Street and Park Avenue
Phone: (212) 818-1777
Comments: Offers free tours centering on the theater district of East 42nd Street on Fridays at 12:30 pm. Sponsored by the Grand Central Partnership.

Times Square Business Improvement District Tour

Address: Tours begin at noon on Friday at the Times Square Visitors Center at 229 West 42nd Street (between Broadway and Eighth Avenue)
Phone: (212) 869-5453
Comments: Aimed at familiarizing visitors with the recent facelift of this famed quarter, the tour meets at noon on Fridays in the heart of the theater district, and they last for about 90 minutes and reveal the lore and architecture of the area. Sponsored by the Times Square Business Improvement District, 212-768-1560.

Urban Park Rangers

Address: Central Park, Crotona Park, Van Cortland Park, Corona Park, Cromwell Recreational Center, and Prospect Park
Phone: Central Park (Manhattan); (212) 988-4952; Crotona Park and Van Cortland Park (The Bronx) (718) 0912; Cromwell Recreational Center (Staten Island), (718) 667-6042; Prospect Park (Brooklyn), (718) 438-0100.
Comments: Found in most major parks throughout the city, this corps of knowledgeable rangers help maintain the parks. They also impart their knowledge to visitors through free tours. Call individual parks for details.

TV Shows

TV shows are free to attend; but getting tickets for some, like David Letterman's, can be nearly impossible. Others, like some of the daytime talks shows, are surprisingly simple to see, and typically take walk-ins. Follow the instructions listed below, and keep in mind that the more popular the show, the less likely it will be to secure a ticket. For popular shows, be prepared to arrive hours in advance for standby tickets.

David Letterman/Late Show

Address: Ed Sullivan Theater, 1697 Broadway (between 53rd and 54th Streets)
Phone: (212) 975-5853
Comments: Mail postcard with name, address and telephone number requesting tickets on desired dates (two tickets are granted per post card) to: Late Show Tickets, 1697 Broadway, New York, NY 10019. Or, wait at theater for standby tickets distributed at 9:00 am on the day of show. Shows are taped Tuesday through Thursday, 1:00 pm through 4:00 pm.

Late Night With Conan O'Brien

Address: 30 Rockefeller Plaza
Phone: (212) 664-3056
Comments: Mail postcard for tickets to: "Late Night With Conan O'Brian," Rockefeller Plaza, New York, NY 10112. Or, try for standby tickets before 9:15 am on day of show at page desk at 30 Rockefeller Plaza (the NBC lobby). Tapings are Tuesday through Friday, **5:30 pm to 6:30 pm.**

Live with Regis and Kathie Lee

Address: ABC Studios at 67th Street and Columbus Avenue
Phone: (212) 456-1000
Comments: For tickets, send a postcard with name, telephone number and address to: Live Tickets, PO Box 777 Ansonia Station, New York, NY 10023. Expect about a 12-month wait. Or, try for standby admission at ABC Studios at 67th Street and Columbus Avenue at 8:00 am on the day of the show.

Maury Povich

Address: 221 West 26th Street
Phone: (212) 989-8800
Comments: Leave message with name, address and telephone number and date requested to reserve two tickets per person. Tickets will be sent.

Montel Williams

Address: 353 West 57th Streets (between Eighth and Ninth Avenues)
Phone: (212) 989-8101
Comments: Write for tickets at: Montel Williams Show, 356 West 58th Street, Room 1001, New York, NY, 10019. Or leave message with name, telephone number and date requested. Or, try for standby tickets at 353 West 57th Streets (between Eighth and Ninth Avenues) Thursday and Friday at 8:45 am.

NBC Today Show

Address: 30 Rockefeller Plaza, 49th Street (between Fifth and Sixth Avenues)
Phone: (212) 664-4249
Comments: Arrive at 6:00 am at the studio. First come, first serve will get admission tickets.

Ricki Lake

Address: 401 Fifth Avenue
Phone: (212) 889-6767
Comments: For tickets, write name, address and date of show requested to: Ricki Lake, 401 Fifth Avenue, New York, NY 10016. Or, try for standby tickets at the studio about an hour before the show Tuesday through Thursday at 4:00 pm through 6:00 pm, when the show is taped.

Rosie O'Donnell

Address: 30 Rockefeller Plaza
Phone: (212) 506-3288
Comments: Very difficult to acquire. Accepting requests during the April-June period for tickets for the following 12-month period. Or, try for standby tickets Monday through Thursday at 8:00 am at the 49th Street entrance to 30 Rockefeller Plaza.

Sally Jessy Raphael

Address: 515 West 57th Street (between Tenth and Eleventh Streets)

Phone: (212) 582-1722
Comments: Either call and reserve tickets, or try for standby tickets on the day of the show at 9:45 am at the studio.

Saturday Night Live
Address: 30 Rockefeller Plaza
Phone: (212) 664-3056
Comments: Holds ticket lottery each August. Mail during that month to: NBC Tickets, "Saturday Night Live," Rockefeller Plaza, New York, NY 10112. Or, try to get tickets at 30 Rockefeller Plaza before 9:15 am on Saturdays.

Victims' Services

New York can be a tough town, but there are a number a places to turn for help, especially for finding referrals ranging from legal assistance to psychological rehabilitation to help in the recovery process.

Crime Victims Assistance Unit, King's County District Attorney's Office
Address: 210 Joralemon Street, Brooklyn Heights
Phone: (718) 250-3820
Comments: Provides counseling on crime prevention and helps victims recover, as well as court information on sexual assault and domestic violence.

Crime Victims Resource Center, New York City Department for the Aging-Elderly
Address: 280 Broadway
Phone: (212) 442-3103
Comments: Primarily dedicated to assisting elderly victims of crime and abuse by providing training and consulting services, as well as referrals.

Family Violence and Child Abuse Bureau, New York County District Attorney's Office
Address: 1 Hogan Place
Phone: (212) 335-4300
Comments: Offers court-related services and social programs to victims of domestic violence.

Rape Crisis Intervention Program, The Mount Sinai Medical Center
Address: 1 Gustave L. Levy Place, Box 1670
Phone: (212) 241-5461
Comments: Aimed at assisting victims of sexual assault through counseling, medical and referral services, all free of charge. Also helps link

survivors with various community and citywide outreach services. Other satellite centers providing similar services include: Metropolitan, North General, Lenox Hill, Harlem, Cabrini, Elmhurst and Queens General Hospitals.

Transition Center

Address: POB 629, Far Rockaway, New York
Comments: Provides free temporary shelter and counseling services to women and children who are victims of rape, child abuse and other forms of abuse. Also offers referrals and childcare.

Victim Services

Address: 2 Lafayette Street, 3rd floor
Phone: (212) 577-7700
Comments: For victims of physical abuse, incest, rape and sexual assault, this agency offers referrals to shelters, and a crime victims' hotline.

Wildlife

The City has a surprisingly large amount of land devoted to wildlife refuge. Though most are in the outer boroughs, they are nevertheless accessible by train or subway. The protected areas draw birds rarely seen elsewhere in the New York area and, hence, a fair number of birdwatchers. Also, many of these refuges have collections of rare plantings and offer a chance to see other animals in natural habitats.

Alley Pond Environmental Center
Address: 228-06 Northern Boulevard, Douglastown, Queens
Open: Tuesday through Friday, 9:00 am to 4:30 pm; Saturday, 9:30 am to 3:30 pm
Phone: (718) 229-4000
Comments: With some 150 acres of wetlands, this Center is primarily an educational outreach program. There are trails for children as well as an aquarium and a small animal room.

Greenbelt, The
Address: 200 Nevada Avenue, Staten Island
Open: Monday through Friday, 10:00 am to 4:00 pm
Phone: (718) 667-2165
Comments: Comprising some 2,500 acres of woods, wetlands and fields, The Greenbelt offers hikers and strollers many trails as well as intriguing glacial formations.

Jamaica Bay Wildlife Refuge
Address: Crossbay Boulevard, Rockaway, Queens
Open: Daily, 8:30 am to 5:00 pm (dawn to dusk)
Phone: (718) 318-4340
Comments: Spread over nearly 9,000 acres of woods and wetlands and water, this free refuge is popular among bird watchers, hikers and children. Birds of over 300 species are spotted through the seasons. Well-maintained trails.

William T. Davis Wildlife Refuge

Address: Travis-Richmond Avenues, New Springville, Staten Island
Phone: (718) 390-8000
Comments: A 260-acre refuge with trails, wetlands, forest, marshes and countless unusual flora and birds.

Women's Groups

There are a number of helpful and accommodating places for women to go for support on a broad range of issues: entrepreneurship, feminist activism, women's studies, health, victimization, and even witchcraft. The selection here is meant more as information to point women in the right direction. Many assist women who don't know where to go for help, and many offer free services like support groups, workshops and consulting, while others may also offer additional services for a fee based on a sliding scale.

American Women's Economic Development Corporation

Address: 71 Vanderbilt Avenue, Suite 320
Phone: (212) 692-9100
Comments: Aims at helping women start businesses. Provides training and counseling to members, but also provides occasional free seminars for non-members. Call for details on free services.

Barnard Center for Research on Women

Address: 101 Barnard Hall, 3009 Broadway
Open: Monday through Friday, 9:30 am to 5:00 pm
Phone: (212) 854-2067
Comments: Holds about 20 events per semester including films, readings, lectures and art exhibitions mainly focusing on women's issues, most are free and open to the public. Also houses an extensive research library. Call for calendar of events or ask for upcoming activities.

Center for the Study of Women and Society

Address: The Graduate School and University Center, CUNY, 33 West 42nd Street
Phone: (212) 642-2954
Comments: Essentially a research group, the society does hold free lectures open to the public, including noon hour brown bag talks. Call for upcoming lectures, which number about six per semester.

Minoan Sisterhood

Address: Events take place at Enchantments, 341 East 9th Street
Phone: (212) 228-4394
Comments: Open only to women, lesbian and straight, this group is dedicated to the Minoan practice of witchcraft. Celebrations and events and training take place from April to October. Meets in the garden of Enchantments.

National Association of Women Business Owners

Address: 234 Fifth Avenue, Suite 403
Phone: (212) 779-7504
Comments: The New York chapter of this group provides support and advocacy for women business owners. Offers networking opportunities and workshops on running a business.

New York University's Womyn's Center

Address: 21 Washington Place, Room 808
Phone: (212) 998-4712
Comments: Sponsors frequent lectures and other cultural events related to women's issues, many of which are free and open to the public.

Women's Center for Education and Career Advancement

Address: 45 John Street, Suite 605
Phone: (212) 964-8934
Comments: Aimed at helping women to find employment through a range of services: personal development and cultural workshops; job listings; and entrepreneurial support services. Also sponsors a free SMART program, dedicated to helping single women parents make the shift to more schooling and/or a job.

WOW (Women's One World Theater)

Address: 59 East 4th Street
Phone: (212) 777-4280
Comments: Meetings hosted by this feminist theater group on Tuesday at 6:30 pm at the WOW Cafe. Call for goings-on.

Zoos

The Bronx Zoo and the Staten Island Zoo welcome visitors free of charge on designated days.

Bronx Zoo

Address: Bronx River Parkway at Fordham Road
Open: Free on Wednesday. April to October: Monday through Friday, 10:00 am to 5:00 pm; Saturday and Sunday, 10:00 am to 5:30 pm. November to March: Monday through Sunday, 10:00 am to 5:00 pm
Phone: (718) 367-1010
Comments: One of the world's most famous zoos, it comprises over 250 acres and houses over 3,500 animals. Includes a dramatic artificial rain forest, including some 100 species of birds, a giraffe house and an elephant house. Free on Wednesdays. Guided tours are free with an appointment.

Staten Island Zoo

Address: 614 Broadway
Open: "Donation Days," Wednesday, 2:00 pm to 4:45 pm
Phone: (718) 442-3100
Comments: Modest zoo with impressive reptiles and fish. Free admission to Children's Zoo, which includes interactive fun with some animals. Wednesdays, known as "Donation Days," which could technically be considered free of charge, though paying nothing would do little for the zoo's financial health.

Miscellaneous

The short list of items below failed to fall neatly into one category, but nevertheless merited inclusion in this book.

Center for Book Arts
Address: 626 Broadway 5th floor (between Bleeker and Houston Streets)
Phone: (212) 460-9768
Comments: Free exhibitions of hand crafted books. Call for times.

Children's Advocacy Center of Manhattan, The
Address: 333 East 70th Street
Phone: (212) 517-3012
Comments: A non-profit, privately financed group dedicated to helping victims of child abuse. Holds free workshops on abuse topics for parents and social workers. Works in tandem with the Police Department, the District Attorney's Office and the Administration for Children's Services in collecting evaluations and evidence. Also offers support groups for adults recovering from physical or sexual abuse as a child.

Directory Assistance from Pay Phones
Phone: 555-1212 or 411
Comments: Phone calls to directory assistance from coin-operated telephones are free in Manhattan. While this service should not be exploited, it does come in handy in emergencies — for example, when you are lost and need an address. Call 555-1212, and politely ask the operator for the address, or the phone number of your destination.

Fencers Club
Address: 154 West 71st Street
Phone: (212) 874-9800
Open: Hours vary, but the club is almost always open from 6:30 pm to 8:30 pm
Comments: The Fencers Club offers free fencing classes on Monday, Wednesday, and to inner-city children on Fridays. Call for details.

General Grant National Memorial

Address: Riverside Drive at West 122nd Street
Phone: (212) 666-1640
Comments: President Ulysses S. Grant's tomb overlooks the river and attracts picnickers in the summer months. The memorial, at 150 feet high, is a dramatic example of Greek Revival architecture and is built of Carrara marble and contains the sarcophagi of the Civil War general and his wife, Julia.

Make-Up, Cosmetics

Most of the finer department stores in the City offer free appointments with cosmetologists who make you over from lips to eyelash. Especially popular are Macy's (151 West 34th Street (212) 695-4400) and Bloomingdale's (1000 Third Avenue (212) 705-2000). Keep in mind that appointments should be scheduled at least two weeks in advance, and that Saturdays are usually packed. Also, it goes without saying that these services are intended for those who are serious about purchasing cosmetic products from these stores.

Staten Island Ferry

Address: Battery Park
Phone: (212) 487-8403 (in Manhattan), (718) 390-5253 (on Staten Island)
Comments: Free ferry transport to and from Battery Park (near Wall Street) to Staten Island's St. George terminal. Spectacular views of the Manhattan skyline.

Steinway & Sons Piano Room

Address: 109 West 57th Street
Open: Monday though Friday, 9:00 am to 6:00 pm
Phone: (212) 246-1100
Comments: The famous Steinway pianos — some 300 of them — are lovingly displayed at Steinway's New York store, an extraordinary spot to visit if you're in the neighborhood. This is sort of half-museum, half-retail shop.

UNICEF House – Danny Kaye Visitors Center

Address: 3 UN Plaza (between First and Second Avenues)
Open: Monday through Friday, 9:00 am to 5:00 pm
Phone: (212) 824-6275
Comments: Changing exhibits focus on UNICEF's efforts around the world to better the plight of children.

Festivals, Fairs & Parades Calendar

New York's abundant street celebrations and marketplaces attract throngs of New Yorkers and tourists alike. Some of these sorts of goings-on are seldom planned for, but the following calendar gives some structure to the year's festivals, fairs and parades, so that readers may actually anticipate visiting them. Remember that dates often vary, so keep an eye out for listings in the newspaper. For literature and a wealth of information, also call the New York Convention and Visitor's Bureau at 212-484-1222.

January

Chinese New Year
Location: Chinatown
End of January
(212) 397-8222

February

Black History Month
Location: Events throughout the City

March

St. Patrick's Day Parade
Location: Fifth Avenue (44th to 86th Streets)
March 17

Greek Independence Day Parade
Location: Fifth Avenue (49th to 59th Streets)
March 25

Easter Parade
Location: Fifth Avenue (44th to 59th Streets)
Easter Sunday

New York Flower Show
Location: Pier 92
The Horticultural Society of New York
(212) 757-0915

Earth Day
Location: Celebrations and street fairs through out the City
Middle of March

Bay Ridge St. Patrick's Day Parade
Location: Brooklyn (Fifth Avenue from 95th to 65th Streets)

Greek Parade
Location: Fifth Avenue (62nd to 79th Streets)
Late March

March-April

Macy's Spring Flower Show
Location: Macy's Department Store at 34th Street
(212) 494-2922

April

Cherry Blossom Festival
Location: Brooklyn Botanic Garden
(718) 622-4433

Gramercy Park Flower Show
Location: Gramercy Park

May

Brooklyn Bridge Day
Location: Brooklyn Bridge
Second week of May

Martin Luther King, Jr. Day Parade
Location: Fifth Avenue (44th to 86th Streets)
Third Sunday in May
(212) 397-8222

Ninth Avenue Street Festival
Location: *(West 37th to 57th Streets)*
Middle of May

Washington Square Outdoor Art Exhibit
Location: *Washington Square Park, Greenwich Village*
Last week of May
(212) 982-6255

You Gotta Have Park
Location: *Events throughout the city's parks*
(212) 360-3456

May-June

Bronx Week Parade
Location: *East Tremont Street*
Late May or Early June

June

Puerto Rican Day Parade
Location: *Fifth Avenue (44th to 86th Streets)*
First week of June

Museum Mile Festival
Location: *Fifth Avenue (82nd to 105th Street)*
Street fair and free Museum admission in mid-June
(212) 535-7710 (Metropolitan Museum of Art)

Metropolitan Opera Parks Concerts
Location:
Free concerts in various parks throughout the city
(212) 362-6000

Gay and Lesbian Pride Day Parade
Location: *Fifth Avenue (Columbus Circle to Washington Square)*
Last week of June
(212) 807-7433

L'eggs Mini-Marathon
Location: *All-women road race starting at 66th Street and Central Park West, ending at Tavern on the Green*
(212) 860-4455 (New York Road Runners Club)

Mermaid Parade
Location: *Coney Island, Brooklyn*
(718) 372-5159

Coney Island Parade
Location: *Steeplechase Park, Brooklyn*
(212) 374-5176

Queens Lesbian and Gay Parade
Location: *Jackson Heights, Queens*
First week of June
(718) 460-4064 (Queens Lesbian and Gay Pride Committee)

Salute to Israel Parade
Location: *Fifth Avenue (52nd to 79th Streets)*
First week of June

Second Avenue Festival
Location:
Street fair first week of June
(212) 576-9000

KIDSDAY
Location: *Brooklyn Historical Society and Brooklyn Public Library*
A family celebration
(718) 624-0890 (Brooklyn Historical Society)

Philippine Independence Day Parade
Location: *Madison Avenue (41st to 26th Streets)*
Mid-June

Feast of St. Anthony Festival
Location: *St. Anthony Church (West Houston and Sullivan Streets)*
Week-long festival, usually first week of June.
(212) 777-2755

June-July

JVC Jazz Festival
Location: *Numerous locales throughout the city*
(212) 501-1390

Buskers Fare Festival
Location: *Street entertainers in venues throughout Lower Manhattan*
(212) 432-0900 (Lower Manhattan Cultural Council)

Washington Square Music Festival
Location: *Washington Square Park, Greenwich Village*

June-August

SummerStage
Location: *Central Park at 72nd Street*
(212) 360-2777

Bryant Park Summer Film Festival
Location: *Sixth Avenue (between 40th and 42nd Street)*
Monday nights
(212) 512-5700

Celebrate Brooklyn Annual Festival
Location: *Prospect Park Bandshell*
Theatre, film, music and dance

New York Philharmonic Park Concerts
Location: *Central Park*
(212) 875-5709

Shakespeare in the Park
Location: *Delacorte Theater, Central Park*
(212) 861-7277

July

Macy's 4th of July Fireworks
Location: *East River*

MacIntosh Music Festival
Location: *Venues throughout Downtown*

July 4th Festival
Location: *Water Street (between State and Fulton Streets)*
Street celebration
(212) 809-4900

August

Harlem Week
Middle of August
Music, art and dance
(212) 862-7200

Indian Day Parade
Location: *Madison Avenue (41st to 26th Streets)*
(212) 374-5176

Brooklyn Puerto Rican Day Parade
(212) 374-5176

Bronx Puerto Rican Day Parade
Location: *East Tremont Avenue to East 161st Street*
First week of August
(212) 374-5176

Pakistan Independence Day Parade and Fair
Location: *Madison Avenue (41st to 26th Streets)*
Late August

August-September

Lincoln Center Out-of-Doors Festival
Location: *Lincoln Center Outdoor Band Shell*
(212) 875-5108

Greenwich Village Jazz Festival
Location: *A one-week festival at venues throughout the Village and a free concert in Washington Square Park*
(212) 691-0045 (International Music Factory)

Brooklyn County Fair
Brooklyn Tourism Council
A one-week fair
(718) 377-4375

September

West Indian Carnival
A Caribbean festival in Brooklyn known for fantastic carnival costumes
Labor Day weekend
(718) 625-1515

One World Festival
Location: *East 35th Street (between First and Second Avenues)*
Second week of September

New York is Book Country
Location: *Fifth Avenue (48th to 59th Streets)*
Book fair

Feast of San Gennaro
Location: *Mulberry Street in Little Italy*
A 10-day Italian neighborhood fair
(212) 226-9546

Von Steuben Day Parade
Location: *Fifth Avenue (61st to 86th Streets)*
German-American Celebration
(516) 239-0741

Wigstock
A festival featuring drag queens
Labor Day
(212) 213-2438

Richmond County Fair
Location: *A county fair in Richmond Town, Staten Island*
Labor Day
(718) 351-1611

Atlantic Antic Street Festival
Location: *Atlantic Avenue, Brooklyn (Flatbush Avenue to Furman Street)*
(718) 875-8993 (Atlantic Avenue Association Local Development Corp.)

Labor Day Parade
Location: *Fifth Avenue (33rd to 72nd Streets)*

Harvest Fair
Location: *Brooklyn Botanic Garden*
A one-day harvest celebration
(718) 622-4433

Broadway on Broadway
Location: *Times Square*
Broadway performers sing tunes from current-running musicals
(212) 768-1560

Third Avenue Festival and Street Fair
Location: *Third Avenue (68th to 96th Streets)*

African American Day Parade
Location: *Adam Clayton Powell Blvd. at 111th Street to 142nd Street to Fifth Avenue*
(212) 374-5176

Korean-American Parade
Location: *41st Street at Broadway and Sixth Avenue to 23rd Street*
(212) 255-6969

African-American/Caribbean Parade
Location: *Bronx (Tremont Avenue to 161st Street)*
(212) 374-5176

October

Columbus Day Parade
Location: *Fifth Avenue (44th to 86th Streets)*

Pulaski Day Parade
Location: *Fifth Avenue (26th to 52nd Streets)*
First week of October

Halloween Parade
Location: *Greenwich Village (Sixth Avenue from Spring Street to Union Square Park)*
October 31st

New York City Marathon
Location: *Through all of NYC's boroughs*
On Sunday, the last week of October or first week of November
(212) 860-4455 (New York Road Runners Club)

Promenade Art Show
Location: *Brooklyn Heights Promenade*
(718) 625-0080 (Brooklyn Arts Council)

Columbus Avenue Festival
Neighborhood festival featuring a wealth of vendors and buskers
(212) 541-8880 (West Side Chamber of Commerce)

Hispanic Day Parade
Location: *Fifth Avenue (44th to 72nd Streets)*
Mid-October
(212) 242-2360

Italian-American Parade
Location: *Brooklyn (18th Avenue from 60th to 82nd Streets)*
(212) 374-5176

Lexington Avenue Oktoberfest
Location: *Lexington Avenue (42nd to 57th Streets)*
First week of October
(212) 809-4900

Avenue of the Americas Family Expo
Location: *Sixth Avenue (43rd to 56th Street)*
Mid-October
(212) 809-4900

Columbus Day Fair
Location: *Downtown Broadway*
Mid-October
(212) 809-4900

Second Avenue Autumn Jubilee
Location:
Mid-October Street fair
(212) 809-4900

November

Macy's Thanksgiving Day Parade
Location: *79th Street and Central Park West to Broadway and 34th Street*

Veterans Day Parade
Location: *Fifth Avenue (39th to 24th Streets)*
(212) 693-1475 (United War Veterans Council)

December

Christmas Tree-Lighting Ceremony
Location: *Rockefeller Center*
An annual tradition lighting of the Christmas tree in front of the RCA Building

Lighting the Hanukkah Menorah
Location: *Brooklyn, Grand Army Plaza*
Eight days of lighting the menorah

New Year's Eve Fireworks
Location: *Central Park*

New Year's Eve Celebration and Ball Drop in Times Square
Location: *Times Square*
Midnight

First Night
Location: *Day and evening New Year's Eve celebrations throughout the City*
(212) 922-9393 (Grand Central Partnership)

Index

34th Street Tours 130
78th Street Theater Lab 127

A

A Different Light 30, 74
A.I.R. Gallery 33
Access for All 115
Ace Gallery New York 34
Actors Studio 127
African -American Day Parade 154
African-American/Caribbean
        Parade 154
Alamo 52
Alianza Dominicana 55
Alice Austen House 81
Alley Pond Environmental
        Center 47, 107, 139
alt.coffee 60
Alternative Spaces 6
American Academy of Arts and
        Letters 117
American Anorexia/Bulimia
        Association 55
American Menopause Foundation,
        Inc. 55
American Museum of Natural
        History 28
American Numismatic
        Society 71, 81, 120
American Stock Exchange 130
American Women's Economic
        Development Corporation
        141
American-Irish Historical Society
        120
Americas Society 120
Anseo 26
Antiquarium, Ltd. 38
Architectural League of New York,
        Urban Center 67

Arlene Grocery 60
Arsenal Gallery 39
Art in General 6
Art Directors Club 82
Art In The Anchorage 74
Arthur's Tavern 60, 102
Artists Space 6, 34
Arts for the Living Center 34
Arts Wire 92
Asia Society 39, 120
Atlantic Antic Street Festival 153
Auction Houses 9
Avenue of the Americas Family
        Expo 155

B

BACA's Summer Celebration 94
BAM/City Parks Outside 94
BAMoutside Music at
        MetroTech 94
Barnard Center for Research on
        Women 71, 141
Barnes & Noble 74
Battery Park City Gardens
        Horticultural Tours 130
Bay Ridge St. Patrick's Day
        Parade 147
Beaches 11
Beekman Tower Hotel 102
Bell Caffe 61
Bellevue Hospital Center 56
Belvedere Castle 99, 107
Bemelmans Bar 103
Benneton's Cafe 75
Bible House 121
Biblio's 75
Big Apple Greeters 115, 131
Bill's Gay 90's 103
Black History Month 146
Black Star 30

Blackout Books 75
Bonni Benrubi 39
Borders Books 75
Brandy's Piano Bar 103
BRC Human Services Corp. 56
Breast Examination Center of
    Harlem 56
Brighton Beach 11
Broadway on Broadway 127, 153
Bronx Council on the Arts 21
Bronx Information and Cultural
    Events 24
Bronx Museum of the Arts 82
Bronx Press Review 111
Bronx Puerto Rican Day
    Parade 151
Bronx Symphony Orchestra 15
Bronx Week Parade 148
Bronx Zoo 143
Brooklyn Arts Council Downtown
    Cultural Center 21
Brooklyn Botanic Garden 47
Brooklyn Bridge Day 147
Brooklyn Children's
    Museum 82, 107
Brooklyn Conservatory of Music 15
Brooklyn County Fair 152
Brooklyn Puerto Rican
    Day Parade 151
Brooklyn Skyliner 111
Brooklyn's History Museum 82
Bryant Park 95, 99
Bryant Park Summer Film
    Festival 30, 150
Bureau of Day Care 108
Bureau of Maternity Services and
    Family Planning, 56
Buskers Fare 95, 150

C

Café Pierre 103
Cancer Information Service 57
Candy Bar & Grill 26
Carpo's Cafe 75
Castillo Cultural Center 21
Castle Clinton Concerts, Battery
    Park 95
Castle Clinton Park 99

Cathedral Church of St. John the
    Divine 15, 113
Cecil's Bar, Crown Plaza Hotel, the
    United Nations 52
Celebrate Brooklyn 96
Celebrate Brooklyn Annual
    Festival 150
Cemeteries 13
Center for Book Arts 144
Center for the Study of Women and
    Society 141
Centerfold Coffeehouse at the
    Church of St. Paul 61
Central Park 96
Central Park, The Arsenal 24
Central Park/ Central Park
    Conservancy 100
Ceres 34
Charles A. Dana Discovery
    Center 108
Cherry Blossom Festival 147
Children's Advocacy Center of
    Manhattan, The 144
Children's Museum of
    Manhattan 109
Children's Museum of the Arts 108
China Institute Gallery 39
Chinese Information & Cultural
    Center 22
Chinese New Year 146
Christie's 9
Christmas Tree-Lighting
    Ceremony 156
Church of St. Lukes in the
    Fields 16
Church of the Transfiguration 16
Ciel Rouge 61, 103
Citicorp Center Public Atrium 117
City Hall 131
City University of New York 67
Classical Music 15
Cloisters, The 47
Cohen Gallery 40
Columbia Presbyterian Center for
    Women's Health 57
Columbia University 67, 131
Columbia University Miller
    Theater 16
Columbus Avenue Festival 155

Columbus Day Fair 155
Columbus Day Parade 154
Comedy 20
Commodities Exchange Center 131
Community Family Planning
        Council 57
Con Edison Energy Museum 83
Coney Island Beach 11
Coney Island Parade 149
Continental Center 16
Cooper Hewitt Museum 83
Cooper Union 68
Cosmetics, Make-Up, 145
Crime Victims Counseling Unit 137
Crime Victims Resource Center 137
Cultural Centers 21
Cultural Information 24
Czech Center 121

D

Dahesh Gallery 40
Dance Clubs and Lounges (No
        Cover DJ) 26
Dance Performances 28
Danny's Skylight Room at the
        Grand Sea Palace 104
Danspace 28
David Geffen Center for HIV
        Prevention and Health 57
David Letterman/Late Show 134
Den of Thieves 26
Department of Cultural Affairs 24
Desmond's Tavern 61
Detour 61
DIA Center for the Arts 7, 76
Directory Asst., Pay Phones 144
Divine Bar 61
Donald Sachs 52
Donnell Library Center 30
Don't Tell Mama 62, 104
Downtown 25
Downtown Express 111
DowntownNY.com 92
Doyle William Galleries 9
Drawing Center, The 34
Druids 62
Duggal Downtown Gallery 35
Duplex Cabaret/Piano Bar/Cafe 104

Dyckman Farmhouse Museum 83

E

E&O 26
Eamon Doran 53
Ear Inn 62
Earth Day 147
Easter Parade 146
Ed Sullivan's Restaurant 62
Eighty-Eight's 104
Elbow Room 62
Eldridge Street Synagogue 113
Eleanor Ettinger Gallery 35
Ellis Island Immigration
        Museum 83
Equitable Center 16
Equitable Gallery 40
Equitable Tower Atrium 117
Exit Art 7

F

Family Violence and Child Abuse
        Bureau 137
Fashion Institute of Technology
        Gallery 121
Fashion Institute of Technology
        Museum 84
Feast of San Gennaro 153
Feast of St. Anthony Festival 150
Federal Hall National Memorial 84
Federal Reserve Bank of New York
        131
Fencers Club 144
Festivals, Fairs & Parades
        Calendar 146
Film 30
First Night 156
Folk Fone 25
Forbes Magazine Galleries 40
Ford Foundation Building 117
Foundation For Hellenic Culture 40
Franklin Furnace 35
Franklin H. Williams Caribbean
        Cultural Center and 22
Fraunces Tavern Museum 109
Free Theater Project 127
French Institute/Alliance
        Francaise 71

Frick Collection 17
Fulcrum Gallery So-Soho 35

G

Gagosian 36, 41
Galleries 32
Gallery Henoch 36
Gallery of Visual Arts, The 36
Garage Restaurant & Cafe 62
Gardens 47
Garibaldi-Meucci Museum, The 84
Gay/Lesbian 50
Gene Frankel Theatre &
        Workshop 128
General Grant National
        Memorial 145
George Gustav Heye Center 85
Gilda's Club 57
GLAAD-NY (Gay and Lesbian
        Alliance) 50
Godel & Co. 41
Goethe House New York 72, 121
Gracie Mansion 132
Grand Hyatt Hotel 63
Grand Tour 133
Great Kills Park Beach 11
Greatest Bar on Earth 27
Grey Art Gallery and Study Center,
        New York 33
Greek Independence
        Day Parade 146
Greek Parade 147
Green Wood Cemetery 13
Greenbelt, The 139
Greenwich Village Jazz Fest 152
Greenwich Village
        Youth Council 109
Grolier Club, The 41

H

HAF 41
Halcyon 104
Halloween Parade 154
Hammer Gallery 41
Hans Christian
        Andersen Statue 109
Happy Hours
        (with free appetizers) 52

Harlem Hospital Saturday Morning
        Screening 58
Harlem Week 151
Harry's Bar 53, 104
Harvest Fair 153
Health Education Center 58
Health Services 55
Hebrew Union College, Jewish
        Institute of Religion 122
Heller Gallery 36
High Rock Conservation Center 48
Himalayan Institute of New York –
        Columbus Avenue 79
Himalayan Institute of New York –
        Fifth Avenue 79
Hirsch & Adler Galleries 42
Hispanic Day Parade 155
Hispanic Society of America 122
Holly Solomon Gallery 36
Hors d'Oeuvres 105
Horticultural Society of
        New York 122
Hotel Galvez 63

I

Identity House 50
Indian Day Parade 151
Institute for Art and Urban
        Resources 122
Interchurch Center 85
International Center of
        Photography 42
Internet Cafe 31
Isamo Noguchi Garden Museum 85
Islamic Cultural Center 113
Italian-American Parade 155

J

Jamaica Arts Center for the
        Performing Arts 22
Jamaica Bay Wildlife Refuge 139
James Graham & Sons 42
Japan House 123
Jazz, Rock & Folk Music 60
Jewish Museum 85
Jewish Theological Seminary 68
Jones Beach State Park 12
Juilliard School 17, 28, 128

Jules 63
July 4th Festival 151
JVC Jazz Festival 150

K

Kenkeleba Gallery 36
Kennedy 42
Kenneth W. Rendell Gallery 43
KGB 76
KIDSDAY 149
Korean Cultural Service 22, 43
Korean-American Day Parade 154
Korean-American Parade 154
Kouros 43
Kurdish Library and
        Museum 72, 86

L

La Galleria Second Class 76
La Table Des Rois 63
Labor Day Parade 153
Lamda Legal Defense and
        Education Fund 50
Langham Leff Gallery 43
Late Night With
        Conan O'Brien 134
Laziza Space 28
Le Parker Meridian Hotel 105
League of American Theaters and
        Producers, Inc. 25
L'ecco Italia 63
Lectures 67
L'eggs Mini-Marathon 149
Lehman College 96
Lenox Hill Bookstore 76
Lenox Lounge 64
Leo Castelli 37
Leonard Hutton 43
Les Poulets 26
Lesbian and Gay Community
        Services Center 50
Lesbian and Gay Pride Day Parade
        148
Lexington Avenue Octoberfest 155
lgny 111
Liberty Lounge, New York Marriott
        Financial Center 105
Libraries 71

Library and Museum of the
        Performing Arts 17, 72
Lighthouse, The 115
Lighting the Hanukkah Menorah
        156
Lincoln Center Out-of-Doors
        Festival 152
Literary Events 74
Live Jazz, Rock & Folk Music 60
Live with Regis and Kathie Lee 134
Lobby Court Lounge, Sheraton New
        York Hotel & Towe 105
Lower East Side Tenement
        Museum 86
Ludlow Bar 27
Ludlow Street Cafe 64
Luna Lounge 20

M

M. Knoedler & Co Inc 44
Macintosh Music Festival 151
Macy's 4th of July Fireworks 151
Macy's Spring Flower Show 147
Macy's Thanksgiving Day Parade
        155
Madison Sculpture Garden 118
Manhattan Beach 12
Manhattan School of Music 17
Manhattan Spirit 111
Mannes College of Music 18
Manny's Car Wash 64
Marco Polo City Listings 92
Marlborough 44
Martin Luther King, Jr.
        Day Parade 147
Mayor's Office for People with
        Disabilities, The 115
Mayor's Office of Film, Theatre and
        Broadcasting 25
Mechanics' and Tradesmen's
        Institute 123
Meditation 79
Mermaid Parade 149
Metronome 64
Metropolitan Opera
        Parks Concerts 148
Mimi Fertz Gallery 37
Minoan Sisterhood 142

Miram and Ira D. Wallach Art
    Gallery 44
Miscellaneous 144
Mitchell's Place 64
Montague Street Saloon 53
Montifiore Medical Center 58
Movement Research at Judson
    Church 29
Municipal Art Society's Urban
    Center 68, 86, 123
Museum Mile Festival 148
Museum of African American
    History and Art 86
Museum of American Financial
    History 87
Museum of Modern Art 31, 87
Museum of Modern Art's
    Summergarden 96
Museums 81

N

National Academy of Design 87
National Alliance of Breast Cancer
    Organizations 58
National Arts Club 32, 76
National Association of Women
    Business Owners 142
New Dramatists 128
New Museum of
    Contemporary Art 68
New School for Social Research 69
New School for Social Research,
    Jazz Division 64
New Year's Eve Celebration and
    Ball Drop 156
New Year's Eve Fireworks 156
New York sidewalk.com 92
New York Academy of
    Medicine 123
New York Academy of Sciences 69
New York Area Bisexual
    Network 51
New York Botanical Garden 48
New York Audubon Society 124
New York City Citysearch 92
    New York City Department of
    Health 58
New York City Marathon 154

New York Comedy Club 20
New York Earth Room 118
New York Flower Show 146
New York Hall of Science 87
New York Historical
    Society 72, 124
New York is Book Country 152
New York Open Center 79
New York Philharmonic 18, 96,
    150
New York Press 111
New York Public Library 77
New York Public Library
    Branches 31
New York Public Library, Center for
    the Humanities 69
New York Public Library for the
    Performing Arts 22
New York Public Library of Science
    and Business 73
New York Public Library: Central
    Research Branch 72
New York Shambhala Center 80
New York Society for Ethical
    Culture 69
New York Society for the Deaf 116
New York Stock Exchange 132
New York Unearthed 88
New York University 69, 77
New York University, Tracey/Barry
    Gallery 32
New York University's Womyn's
    Center 142
New York Web 92
News Communications, Inc. 111
Newseum/NY 88
Nicholas Roerich Museum 88
Ninth Avenue Street Festival 148
North Shore Animal League 101
Nuyorican Poets Cafe 77
NV 27
NYCInsider 93
NYC Poetry Calendar 77
NYC Tours 132
NYC Web Sites 92

O

Oak Room, The Plaza Hotel 105

Oaks Piano Bar and Restaurant 105
One World Festival 152
Open Center Meditation Room 118
Opium Den 27
Orchard Beach 12
Orchard Street Shopping District Tour 132
Ottendorfer Library 31, 110
Our Town 111
Out-of-Doors Festival 96
Outdoor Performances 94

P

P.S. 1 Museum 7
PaceWildenstein 44
Paine Webber Art Gallery 45
Pakistan Independence Day Parade and Fair 152
Parks 99
Peacock, The 77
PEN American Center 124
Perry Art Gallery 37
Pets 101
Philippine Independence Day Parade 149
Piano Bars 102
Places for Children 107
Players Sports Bar, The New York Hilton and Towers 53
Poetry Society of America 78
Poets House 78
Police Academy Museum 88
Positive Health Project 58
Pratt Manhattan 37
Promenade Art Show 154
Prospect Park 97, 100
Publications 111
Puerto Rican Day Parade 148
Pulaski Day Parade 154

Q

Queens Botanical Garden 48
Queens Council on the Arts 23
Queens County Farm Museum 89
Queens Historical Society 124
Queens Lesbian & Gay Parade 149
Queen's Tribune 111

R

Rape Crisis Intervention 137
Regents 106
Religious Buildings 113
Resources for the Disabled 115
Restful Places 117
Richmond County Fair 153
Riverside Church 114
Rockaway Beach 12
Rockefeller Center 133
Rose's Turn 106
Ryan's Irish Pub 65

S

S.E. Feinman Fine Arts 38
Salmagundi Club 89
Salute to Israel Parade 149
Saturday Night Live 136
Savoy Lounge 65
Sazerac House 65
Schomberg Center for Research in Black Culture 125
School of Visual Arts Museum 89
Sculptors Guild 38
Sculpture Center 45
Second Avenue Autumn Jubilee 155
Second Avenue Festival 149
Senor Swanky's 53
Seuffert Bandshell 97
Seventh Regiment Armory 89
Shades of Lavender 51
Shakespeare & Co. 78
Shakespeare in the Park 128, 151
Shakespeare in the Parking Lot 128
SHARE: Self-Help for Women with Breast or Ovarian 59
Skyscraper Museum 90
Snug Harbor Cultural Harbor 23
Societies & Institutes 120
Society of Illustrators 45, 124
Socrates Sculpture Park 48
Solo Arts Club 20
Solomon R. Guggenheim Museum 90
Sony Wonder Technology Lab 110
Sophia's 65
Sotheby's 10

Sounds at Sunset at the Battery Park Esplanade 97
Sounds on the Hudson 97
South Street Seaport Museum 90
South Street Seaport/Pier 17 97
Spanish Institute, The 125
St. Bartholomew's Church 114
St. Mark's-in-the-Bowery 129
St. Patrick's Cathedral 18, 114
St. Patrick's Day Parade 146
St. Paul's Chapel 18
St. Paul's Churchyard 13, 118
Staten Island Botanical Garden 100
Staten Island Children's Museum 110
Staten Island Economic Development Corporation 25
Staten Island Ferry 145
Staten Island Zoo 143
Statue of Liberty National Monument and Museum 91
Steinway & Sons Piano Room 145
Storefront for Art and Architecture 7
SummerMusic, Bronx Arts Ensemble 98
SummerStage 98, 150
Swann Galleries 10
Swing 46 65
Swiss Institute 125

T

T.G. Whitney's 54
Taipei Gallery 45
Tatou 53
Teachers and Writers Collaborative 78
Teddy's Bar and Grill 65
Temple Emanu-El 114
Tepper Galleries 10
Terrace at Blue Cross Center 118

Theater 127
Theaterworks/USA 129
Third Avenue Festival and Street Fair 153
Third Street Musical School

Settlement 18
Thread Waxing Space 8
Time Square Business Improvement District Tour 133
Tours 130
Toyota Comedy Festival 20
Transition Center 138
Trinity Church 13, 18, 114
Trinity Church Graveyard 118
TV Shows 134

U

Ukrainian Institute of America 125
UN Plaza-Park Hyatt 106
UNICEF House – Danny Kaye Visitors Center 145
Union Square Summer Series 98
United Nations Garden 49, 118
Urban Park Rangers 133

V

Van Allen Institute 126
Van Cortlandt Park 100
Veterans Day Parade 155
Veterinary Hospitals 101
Victims' Services 137, 138
Village Comics 78
Village Voice 93, 112
Visiones 66
Visual Arts Museum 33
Void 27, 31
Von Steuben Day Parade 153

W

Waldorf-Astoria Hotel 106
Washington Square Music Festival 98, 150
Washington Square Outdoor Art Exhibit 148
Washington Square United Methodist Church 29
Water Street Plaza 119
Wave Hill Center for Environmental Studies 49
West Bank Cafe 129
West Indian Carnival 152
White Columns 8

Whitney Museum at Philip Morris
        91
Whitney Museum of American Art
        91
Wigstock 153
Wildenstein 46
Wildlife 139
William T. Davis Wildlife Refuge
        140
Winter Garden, World Financial
        Center 119
Witkin Gallery 38
Women's Center for Education and
        Career Advancement 142
Women's Groups 141
Women's Health Forum 59
Woodlawn 14
World Financial Center Arts &
        Events Program 19, 38
World Trade Center 19
WOW (Women's One World
        Theater, 142
Writer's Voice, The 78

Y

YIVO Institute For Jewish
Research 126
Young DanceMakers Company 29
You Gotta Have Park 148

Z

Zoos 143
Zuni 66

Special Note

The publisher invites readers of this book to contribute any suggestions for changes or new entries.

Please mail to:
Tatra Press, 111 Congress Street, Brooklyn, New York 11201
Much thanks.

NOTES